Toronto Women

Toronto Women

Changing Faces 1900-2000

A Photographic Journey

Photographic Research by

Jeanne MacDonald and Nadine Stoikoff

Text by

Randall White

To Rob's favourite
Toronto Woman

Nadine Stoikoff

Jeanne MacDonald

eastendbooks
Toronto 1997

Designed by Andy Tong

Printed in Canada by Metrolitho

Front cover: *Toronto Women* illustration © Andrew Judd
Back cover: On the waterfront at Fisherman's Island, City of Toronto Archives, William James Fonds, SC 244-177
On the waterfront at Balmy Beach, Susanne Milligan, Photographer

Canadian Cataloguing in Publication Data

MacDonald, Jeanne, 1943–
Toronto women : changing faces: 1900–2000

Includes bibliographical references and index.
ISBN 1-896973-04-3

1. Women – Ontario – Toronto – History – 20th century – Pictorial works.
I. Stoikoff, Nadine. II. White, Randall. III. Title.

HQ1460.T6W44 1997 305.4'09713'5410904 C97-932004-6

eastendbooks is an imprint of Venture Press
45 Fernwood Park Avenue
Toronto, Canada
M4E 3E9
(416) 691-6816 [telephone]
(416) 691-2414 [fax]

Contents

Acknowledgements 6

INTRODUCTION: The Gendered Passage 9

1 AGE OF INNOCENCE 17
2 STORM CLOUDS 31
3 ANYTHING GOES 43
4 AND THE BAND PLAYED ON 59
5 WHAT A LOVELY WAR 75
6 AT THE EDGE OF CHANGE 91
7 THE NEW METROPOLIS 105
8 ON THE CUSP 121

EPILOGUE: Megacity PMS 137

Select Bibliography 142
Index of Photographs 143

Acknowledgements

Any enterprise that celebrates the role played by women in shaping the life of a metropolis as large as Toronto today, over as long a period as an entire century, is bound to accumulate some stupendous debts.

Apart from the photographs themselves, we are deeply indebted to the talent and enthusiasm of Andrew Judd, who managed to create just the kind of art we wanted for the cover of the book, on time and in good cheer. And we should note that what lies between the covers would not look as attractive as it does without the patient skill and craftsmanship of our designer, Andy Tong.

We have received a great deal of help from some excellent people at the old city of Toronto (or the one now being superseded by the new megacity of 1998). David Whorley, Pamela Wachna, and Joanne Licursi have been more than generous with their time and valued support. And Angela Trunfio has introduced us to the Mayor's photograph collection.

The city of Toronto archives staff Glenda Williams, Karen Teeple, Elizabeth Cuthbertson, Linda Price, and Steve MacKinnon provided endless assistance. In the central records section, Ken Romanada, Peter Tassiopoulos, Peter Goodwin, Zerezghi Haile, and Farhad Khadim assisted endlessly as well (and introduced us to the best restaurants within walking distance of city hall). Jocelyn Richards patiently developed dozens of photographs. Sandra Pinto provided important information on economic development. And Ron Mitchell, who presides over underground operations, makes everyone's life more agreeable.

At the old North York city hall, we received a great deal of help as well from Sheila White in the Mayor's office, and from Lalitha Flach and Mark Cuddy in the corporate records office. In still other quarters, we are indebted to the kind assistance of: Alan Walker, archivist for special collections at the Metropolitan Toronto Reference Library; Linda Cobon and Amber Timmons, at the CNE Archives; and Gabe Scardellato and Reneé Rogers at the Multicultural History Society of Ontario.

The photographs covering the first half of the twentieth century in our collection are almost exclusively drawn from archival sources. Our approach to the last fifty years has necessarily been more eclectic. To start with, a number of women have kindly provided personal photographs. We would like to express our gratitude to Rosalie Abella, Rella Braithwaite, Raynette Coker, Amina Guled, Isobel Hoffmann, Betty Kennedy, Marilyn Lastman, Suhana Meharchand, Barbara Elizabeth Mercer, and Paris Quinn.

Alex MacDonald, who has been taking photographs of Toronto women since the late 1960s, generously put his private collection at our disposal, and patiently shot some additional pictures on our behalf. The last two chapters of the book have been notably shaped by his handiwork. We are indebted in a similar connection to the work of photographers Anne Bayin, Natalie MacFarlane, and Susanne Milligan.

We are grateful as well for the good offices of Marion Byard of the Ontario Black History Society, Tim Casey, Paget Catania, Dana Davis of the Court of Appeal for Ontario, Rashid Farrah, Stephen Haines and Ceridwyn Howard of Hoffman and Associates, Liz Martin of Second Story Press, Vince Papa of Mediawerx Creative Group, Colleen Pollreis of the *Toronto Star*, Michael Seward, and Bryan Vaughan — all of whom either provided photographs from their own private collections, or helped us secure photographs from other sources. In a related connection here, we would like to thank both *Chatelaine* magazine for providing a photograph, and Carolyn Chua, Breda Harding, Monda Rosenberg, and Evelyn Stoynoff for helping to identify the individuals in the picture involved.

More than a few other people have provided less direct but quite crucial assistance. For important information on specific photographs we are indebted to: Dawn Andrews of the Metropolitan Toronto Police Amateur Athletic Association, historian Lesley Barsky, Keri Bishop of the Canadian Olympics Association, Rodney Bobiwash of First Nations House, Wendy Harker of the Women's Christian Temperance Union, Heather Howard of the Native Canadian Centre, Susan McGrath of the Toronto Board of Education, Ed Patrick of the Toronto Press Club, Stephen Speisman of the Canadian Jewish Congress Ontario Region Archives, and Andrea Thom of the Toronto Argonauts organization.

Rand Paterson of Transcontinental Printing and art project specialist Suzanne Linds have provided special technical support. Frieda Forman of the Women's Educational Resource Centre at the Ontario Institute for Studies in Education was helpful during early phases of the research. For more diffuse forms of valued assistance and support we are grateful to Jane Anderson, Joe Bohonos, Peter Carruthers, Eileen Craig, Michelle Drover, Joanne Green, Marita Hollo, David Mauti, Melissa McClelland, Marcia McVea, Stan Michna, David Montgomery, Donna Montgomery, Kathy O'Reilly, Jean Paton, Rob Piltch, Susan Piltch, David Ross, Gertrud Schneider, Janet Sherbanowski, Marie Sibley, Dyan Starr, and Judith Turnbull. And we would also like to thank the Bank of Montreal, particularly Kimberley Van Der Zon and Lynne Mallatratt, for their generous help in promoting *Toronto Women*; and the city of Toronto for making available the Market Gallery for the introduction of the book.

Almost last, but by no means least at all, is a very big thank you for Gordon Tucker, who has helped us in so many ways that he deserves a paragraph of his very own.

Given the subject of the book, it may be appropriate as well to express our special gratitude to our mothers, Gertrude Lindsay MacDonald, Menka Lumanis Stoikoff, and Louise Craig Reynolds, along with our assorted alphabetically ordered children — Jason Edmunds, Alicia Mauti, Joe White, William White, and Matthew Williams. But, most of all, we would like to acknowledge our enormous debt to all the women, named and unnamed, whose photographs appear in the pages that lie ahead.

J.M.
N.S.
R.W.

Toronto
September 1997

WOMEN PHOTOGRAPHERS, TORONTO NORMAL SCHOOL, 1922. The Normal School, on Gould Street, first erected in 1851 and remodelled in 1896, housed the local teachers' college for many years. It was also something of a centre for one side of the city's cultural life — as is the present-day institution that has inherited the real estate involved, Ryerson Polytechnic University. Just why these particular Toronto women photographers were in attendance in 1922 remains a minor mystery. What we do know is that some 33 percent of all city of Toronto high-school teachers were women in 1920 (and 50 percent would be women some seventy-five years later, in 1996).

City of Toronto Archives (CTA), William James Family Fonds (WJF), SC 244-101.31

Introduction

THE GENDERED PASSAGE

The first point to clarify is how a book that covers the historical time period, 1900–2000, can be published in 1997. And the answer is that this is a book of photographs of women who have lived in the Toronto metropolis during the twentieth century. Barring some millennial cataclysm over the next few years, a number of the women who live in these photographs will still be living in Toronto in the year 2000.

The strategy for selecting the photographs has, frankly, been eclectic. Toronto has had its share of rich and/or famous and/or beautiful women, and we have had some concern to give them their space. It has also had its share of officially obscure members of what Simone de Beauvoir (quite some time ago now) cleverly called the "the second sex." We have been at least equally concerned to give them their space as well.

The premise of the book is that women have made an enormous contribution to Toronto life in the twentieth century, and that this contribution deserves to be celebrated as the century comes to its end. Our working assumption has been that excuses for such a celebration are not strictly necessary. But for those who may want reasons, one possible candidate is the unasked-for new political era that will be brought on by the advent of the Ontario provincial government's dreaded "megacity" in 1998.

In a more important sense, the most authentic virtues of Toronto in the twentieth century have had a lot to do with its female inhabitants. *Fortune* magazine in the USA has recently informed its readers that this is a city where "you can perform great work" and "also have a life ... a good place for raising a family." In fact "internationally, no other metropolitan area combines favorable working and living conditions as well as Toronto." On *Fortune's* calculations, Toronto's rivals among the world's "best cities for work and family" include London, Singapore, Paris, and Hong Kong. But Toronto is at the top of the list. And even in the age of liberation, it seems correct enough to say that the women of Toronto have played an indispensable role in winning this prize.

A few introductory words about how both Toronto and its women managed to arrive at the start of the twentieth century are no doubt in order, as background to the photographs themselves.

The local boosters of an earlier era conveniently discovered that Toronto was an Iroquoian or, more exactly, Huron word, that supposedly meant "place of meeting" or perhaps "place of plenty." The more recent and intellectually rigorous research of Mr. John Steckley, a Huron language expert at Humber College, suggests that the real meaning of the word is closer to "trees in water." And this may have something to do with an observation of the late eighteenth-century visitor, Joseph Bouchette, about the "dense and trackless forests" which once "lined the margin of the lake" in what is now Toronto harbour, and "reflected their inverted images in its glassy surface."

Whatever the exact meaning of the word, there have been people living in the place for thousands of years. An archaeological report in the 1970s identified more than 190 sites of "prehistorical settlements" in the "Metropolitan Toronto area," a few of which can be dated as far back as 5000 BC. Apparently, the Iroquoian peoples who had the most to do with Toronto immediately before and after the arrival of Europeans first moved to the north shore of Lake Ontario around AD 1000. They probably deserve some special mention in any book about Toronto women as well: Iroquoian society was "matrilineal," tracing descent through women rather than men.

In the mid- to late-seventeenth century, there were two Iroquois villages near the mouths of what are now called the Humber and Rouge rivers. These villages exploited the area's location at the foot of a long canoe portage between the upper and lower Great Lakes of North America. This is the almost mystical "Toronto Passage" of ancient legend, and its strategic geography still haunts the present in such forms as Yonge Street and Highway 400. Figuratively, at least, the passage has always been Toronto's pathway to the riches of the great northern North American wilderness (or, a cynic from Montreal might say, what finally turned Toronto into New York City's principal outpost in the vast Canadian hinterland).

The same strategic attractions of the Toronto Passage had lured a modest French trading post to the area in the 1720s — followed by a modest French fort in the 1750s. By this time, the Mississauga had supplanted the Iroquois on the north shore of Lake Ontario. And for another generation after what is still known in French as "la conquête" (or the Seven Years' War, 1756–1763), Toronto was an intermittent way station for various mixed groups of North American aboriginal, European, and other peoples, principally concerned with the fur trade in Canada — the rugged, romantic, and quite culturally diverse first chapter in the story of the modern Canadian resource economy.

Probably the best-known Toronto trader of the later eighteenth century is Jean Baptiste Rousseau — also called "Mr. St. John of St. John's Creek." Rousseau had parted company with his first wife, Marie Martineau, and sometime around 1787 married Margaret Clyne, the adopted daughter of the Mohawk British empire loyalist Joseph Brant. Margaret was a woman of great spirit, locally famous for having once paddled a canoe along the north shore of Lake Ontario, all the way from what we call Hamilton to Kingston today.

In the summer of 1793 Toronto took another step towards a new kind of future. The exuberant Lieutenant Governor John Graves Simcoe pulled into the harbour, shook hands with "Mr. St. John," and established the British North American town of York. Somewhat accidentally, the town of York became the capital of the new British imperial province of Upper Canada. (And Toronto, of course, remains the capital of the Canadian successor province of Ontario today.) At first Simcoe and his wife, Elizabeth, lived in an enormous canvas tent, said to have once belonged to Captain Cook. Elizabeth nowadays seems to have been a rather more sensible person than her husband. She has bequeathed an interesting diary and some drawings of her quite brief sojourn on the site of the present-day Toronto metropolis. According to legend, when she left the place forever, in the summer of 1796, she cried all day.

The earliest growth of what the Simcoes left behind was not dramatic. At the outbreak of the War of 1812, there were still fewer than one thousand people living in the town of York. Then in the 1820s, migrants from the United Kingdom began to descend upon the place, and it started to grow towards its present state. In 1834 the town of York became a city, and changed its name back to Toronto. In 1836 the new city was home to just under ten thousand people. They included the "British gentlewoman," Anna Jameson, whose *Winter Studies and Summer Rambles in Canada* paints what the present-day Torontonian Clara Thomas has called "a lively but uncomplimentary portrait of Toronto" — on the eve of William Lyon Mackenzie's failed but nonetheless influential Upper Canada Rebellion of 1837.

Ms. Jameson's well-composed harsh words apparently did not convince all her compatriots across the ocean that Toronto was a city to avoid. By the middle of the nineteenth century, the old capital of Upper Canada had become something of a notoriously "*British* American" place — a magnet for a wide variety of migrants from various parts of the United Kingdom, and a confirmed new-world outpost of the global empire on which the sun never set. Some 60 percent of Toronto's thirty thousand inhabitants in 1851 had been born in the United Kingdom, 34 percent in Canada, and 6 percent in other places. It was still true that close to a bare majority of Toronto women and men alike had been born in the UK, even at the time of the Canadian confederation in 1867.

In the later nineteenth century, the city's growth would start to draw on other sources. The capital of what was even then Canada's most populous province was rapidly becoming its principal economic metropolis as well. In fact, the first generation of the Canadian confederation had proved to be something of an economic struggle. But Toronto had, nonetheless, seriously begun its extended career as a rising centre of commerce, finance, and manufacturing. It attracted increasing numbers of domestic Canadian migrants from the small towns and rural areas of the Ontario countryside. And while the population of Ontario at large grew very little, Toronto blossomed from a rather small city of fifty-six thousand people in 1871 into a considerably more bustling proto-metropolis of more than 181,000 in 1891.

By the 1890s, other kinds of more various growth were at least very gently rustling in the breeze. In *Canada and the Canadian Question* (first published in 1891), Toronto's resident English intellectual, Goldwin Smith, noted that, though "the British" were certainly dominant in the area, there were also "scatterings of other races, the last arrival being the Italian." The city of Toronto actually elected its first black alderman, William Peyton Hubbard, in 1894 (though at this time the city's black community was sometimes said to number no more than "one hundred families"). The 1901 census of Canada reported that 73 percent of Toronto's population had been born in Canada, 21 percent in the United Kingdom, and 6 percent in other places. It also gave some evidence of new Jewish arrivals from eastern Europe, and a few hundred new Chinese labourers, many of whom had apparently worked on the construction of the Canadian Pacific Railway, which was completed in 1885.

Some partial but still provocative census data from the late nineteenth century suggests that women had begun to show their own kind of dominance on the Toronto scene as well. Men had significantly outnumbered women in the early 1830s, during the dying days of the old town of York. But the situation was reversed by the middle of the nineteenth century. And the reversal seems to have grown somewhat more pronounced as the nineteenth century marched to its conclusion. Incomplete data from the 1901 census suggests that for every 100 men in Toronto, there were as many as 114 women. It's at this point that our own photographs of Toronto women begin. And while they are meant in the first instance as no more than an entertainment, they probably do say something about the deeper story of both Toronto and its women, in the twentieth century that lay ahead.

Back at the present day, when the twentieth century is about to end, there are some inevitable housekeeping issues in any project of this sort. How you choose to deal with these issues has a bearing on the shape your photograph collection assumes. And this, too, deserves some brief introductory comment.

To start with, the establishment of the new Toronto megacity raises the question of exactly what chunk of geographic space is covered by our photographs of Toronto women. Even the city of Toronto in its narrowest legal sense occupied rather less geographic space at the start of the twentieth century than it would later on. Various vaguer concepts of "greater Toronto" have been in the air virtually throughout the century.

Our practice in selecting photographs of Toronto women has been to stick to the prevailing view of what "Toronto" meant when the photograph was taken — without being too inhibited by the narrowest official definitions on the one hand, or too extravagant about reaching further afield on the other. From here, we have taken a "Toronto woman" to be any female who has lived somewhere inside our flexible-but-not-too-flexible concept of Toronto geography, for some significant part of her life.

We have preferred, wherever possible, to identify the people who appear in the photographs by including names. We have tried to be scrupulous about not identifying anyone unless we were quite confident that she is or was the person named, and that we had some fairly clear idea of how to spell her name properly. Yet in the nature of things, the materials we have worked with are frequently less than perfect, and there is inevitably some room for error. All we can finally say is that we have taken great pains to be as accurate as possible, and (as the publishers' optimistic jargon has it) we welcome information that may lead to "any necessary corrections in future editions."

Putting together a photographic collection of this sort also raises some questions about time, as well as geographic space. Should the photographs be arranged in exact chronological sequence, for example, and should the collection at large be more or less evenly distributed across the entire time period, from 1900 to the present day?

One relevant feature of the materials at our disposal here is that — as in the case of so many private photograph collections — it has not always been possible to date the available pictures exactly. Thus, even if one wanted to arrange all of them in exact chronological sequence, it could never be done with confidence. What we have done is divide the book into eight broadly chronological chapters. Within each of the eight chapters we have been somewhat less concerned again to follow a strictly chronological or precisely dated regime. But we have remained interested in preserving some sense of the fabled march of time.

The question of whether the photographic collection at large should be more or less evenly distributed across the entire period, from 1900 to the present day, raises some special problems. In the course of our research, one of our favourite Toronto women bookstore managers advised us that it is the older rather than the more recent pictures which most seem to attract readers to the kind of book we have tried to create here.

It may be, our advisor speculated, that the more recent photographs are just too much like what we already see every day, beyond our own front doors, to hold real fascination. And this may also have something to do with the near-famous remark of the earlier nineteenth-century philosopher, George Wilhelm Frederich Hegel: "Minerva's owl begins its flight only in the gathering dusk." We cannot really understand an era in time until it has ended, and the more recent past has not yet come to an end.

At the same time, particularly in the late twentieth century, older photographs close to home can create problems of their own. Not all that long ago, the Ottawa writer Jean Bruce noted that the photographic and other material she collected for her 1985 book on *Canadian Women During the Second World War*

> provides the context and the atmosphere of a period not very far removed in time from the 1980s, but quite "foreign" in spirit in many ways. The attitudes towards the war itself, towards the British connection, towards the role of women in the family unit, will strike the modern reader as very different, although other things may seem surprisingly contemporary ... But beware: the way these women thought, wrote, and behaved has to be considered in the context of their time, not ours, if we want to understand their point of view.

Put another way, there has been a kind of sea change in the twentieth-century life of places like Toronto — in various parts of the global village. Viewed from one angle, the entire century is about accumulating changes that finally start to reach a new fruition somewhere in the 1960s or beyond. From another angle, the earlier parts of the century are about the endings of an old story, and the more recent past is about the beginnings of a new one. Beginnings are always less tidy and more confused than endings. And if the later parts of our photographic exploration of Toronto women here do in fact seem somewhat less tidy and more confused than the earlier parts, we invite readers to contemplate the prospect that this is not entirely our fault.

We should finally say a few short words of more particular introduction about the public and private sources from which our photographs have been drawn.

The best place to start here is the not-at-all-well-enough-known career of the incomparable John Boyd — first staff photographer for the old Toronto *Globe* (now known as the *Globe and Mail*) and a man who very much liked women, in the best (and perhaps a few of the worst) senses of these words. His complete photographic works, as it were, cover the period from just after the First World War to a point rather longer after the Second World War. They are now appropriately stored in the City of Toronto Archives (in the old sense of this term, for students of the coming megacity), and they have served as the initial seminal inspiration for this book.

Once we had decided to explore Toronto women in the twentieth century at large, we had to find photographs from periods both before and after the incomparable John Boyd. Our main solution for the earliest years of the twentieth century has been to plunder the riches of the William James photographic collection, also stored at the present City of Toronto Archives.

There is something of a contrast between the James photographs (which dominate Chapters 1 and 2) and the pictures taken by Boyd (which dominate Chapters 3, 4, and 5, and at least figure somewhat significantly in parts of Chapter 6 as well). And this contrast probably has something to do with the rather different backgrounds that Boyd and James brought to their work.

John Boyd was born in 1898 in Sarnia, Ontario, to a John Boyd, Sr., who was also interested in photography, but earned his living at a job with what ultimately became Canadian National Railways. In pursuit of railway business, the Boyd family moved to Toronto towards the end of the First World War. John Boyd spent some time at Parkdale Collegiate, not long before he became the *Globe*'s first staff photographer in the early 1920s. And he is looking at Toronto women, among other things, through the eyes of someone who moved to the city from southwestern Ontario in his late teens.

William James, on the other hand, was born in England in 1866, and did not migrate to Toronto until 1906 (when he was already forty years old). He had been a mere "photo-hobbyist" in England. But he managed to establish himself as a professional photographer only a few years after his arrival in Toronto, and ultimately did a lot of freelance work for what was then called the *Toronto Daily Star*. He is looking at Toronto women through the eyes of a migrant from across the ocean, who achieved a certain personal salvation through the act of emigration, in his middle age.

In fact, it seems clear enough that some of the later pictures in the Boyd collection at the city archives were taken by assistants under Boyd's direction, rather than by the master himself. But in a much more decisive sense, no single person at the camera dominates Chapters 6, 7, and 8 of the book, in at all the same way as John Boyd and William James dominate their respective portions of the earlier parts. We have, nonetheless, been fortunate in securing access to quite a wide variety of other public and private photograph collections. Our galaxy of debts in this and other respects are catalogued extensively in the Acknowledgements that appear at the start of the book.

To help compensate for our various presumptions on the local public spirit, in this and other respects again, in an epilogue at the end of the photograph collection we have indulged in some gratuitous speculations on what we ourselves think we have learned from gazing at all the pictures of Toronto women in this book, and what this might mean for the current great debate on the megacity, and all that. Many may not be interested, and they should, of course, just ignore our exertions here. But another friend advised us that: "You can't do any kind of book on Toronto right now without saying something about the megacity." And we have concluded that this, too, was good advice.

JOHN BOYD AND HIS FIANCÉE, MARJORIE LANG, SANDY POINT, JUNE 1925. In many ways the twentieth century, especially in North America north of the Rio Grande (or, as the Rio Grande is known in Mexico, "Bravo del Norte"), has been the age of the automobile. And, while Toronto's immediate geography is not all that impressive, there are more intriguing places, closer to the northern North American wilderness, that can be easily reached by car. John Boyd, who grew up in Ontario, outside Toronto itself, took many photographs of such places. He and Marjorie Lang were married in the 1930s and had a daughter, Joan. They eventually settled in what is now Etobicoke, not too far from Boyd's parents, who lived in the older west end of the city, near High Park.

CTA, Globe and Mail Fonds (G&M), SC 266-5674-G

ON THE WATERFRONT AT FISHERMAN'S ISLAND
(east side of Eastern Gap, foot of Cherry Street), Toronto, ca. 1907.
CTA, WJF, SC 244-177

1 *Age of Innocence*

No less an authority than the visiting Walt Whitman had enthused about the "pretty view of Toronto from the blue foreground" of Lake Ontario in 1880. But the railway building of the later nineteenth century had already begun to destroy the city's waterfront when the twentieth century first dawned. Even so, in the early 1900s the lake, and especially "the Islands" (created from what was originally "the Peninsula" during a great storm in 1858), played a much bigger role in Toronto life than they do today.

The exact identity of the three young women in the water here remains another minor mystery. We, nonetheless, do know that the "city proper" — as it was said in those days — was home to a mere 208,040 people in 1901. At the start of the twentieth century, Toronto was still only Canada's second most-populous city, after Montreal (a locally lamented circumstance that would not change until the middle of the 1970s).

In 1901 well over half the people in Toronto were women. In central Canada, generally, at the time, urban centres tended to have more women, while rural townships had more men. The family farm was still a great bulwark of the regional economy, but it seems that it was never all that attractive to the female of the species. Women moved disproportionately to urban centres, to take advantage of new opportunities and new ways of life. For all the surrounding countryside, Toronto had the brightest city lights.

After an arduous generation of economic transition and frustration, in the late 1890s Canada at large at last stumbled into the great boom that would launch the country's modern "take-off" to the fast lane of global economic growth. The city of Toronto joined the trend with resolute enthusiasm and annexed several chunks of its surrounding geography in 1906, 1908, 1909, 1910, and 1912. Yet much of the texture of city life retained some earlier innocence. In the wider world of which Canada is a part, it is often said, the nineteenth century did not really end until the First World War. When you look at the earliest photographs of Toronto women in the twentieth century, you seem to see some similar force at work — a kind of agreeably naïve last, long picnic, at the water's edge.

ALICE DINNICK, WIFE OF AUGUSTUS GEORGE DINNICK, EARLY 1900s. The great Canadian boom of the early twentieth century brought new prosperity to more than a few rising young men in Toronto. The casualty insurance executive Augustus Dinnick was one of them. In 1905 he decided that he could at last afford a wife who was accustomed to a certain style. He married Alice Benson, a young lady of some position from the Channel Islands, and she quickly joined the ranks of the more fortunate among the Toronto women of her day. A few years later, the Dinnicks were living in the Deer Park neighbourhood near St. Clair and Yonge, with two small sons.

Metropolitan Toronto Reference Library, 977-20-3

IMMIGRANT WOMAN AND CHILD, MID-1900s. The great new boom also attracted many migrants in less-fortunate circumstances than Alice Dinnick to Toronto. As in the nineteenth century that had just ended, the overwhelming majority still came from the United Kingdom. Unprecedented numbers of Jewish migrants from eastern Europe also began to arrive in the first decade of the twentieth century, however, along with small numbers of Italians and (smaller still) Chinese. The exact origin and even the names of the immigrant woman and child here are unknown, but they are likely enough from the United Kingdom. The look on the woman's face suggests something of the fatigue of a long journey by ocean liner (and finally by railway car, from which the pair in this photograph have just emerged).

CTA, WJF, SC 244-83.36

THE YWCA'S "ONTARIO HOUSE," MID- TO LATE-1900s. There was still considerable migration to Toronto from other parts of Ontario in the early twentieth century. And the best evidence is that these Toronto women are descendants of the "African Americans" who had fled to various southwestern parts of the province on the fabled underground railway, during the earlier nineteenth century. They, too, have come to the booming big city to seek better lives. At the time, the Young Women's Christian Association operated seven homes for such newly arrived "business and industrial girls in different parts of the city." This one on Ontario Street, according to an early historian of the YWCA in Canada, was specifically "for coloured girls with living accommodations, sitting and reading rooms." Toronto's black community would remain quite small until much later in the new century. But it did exist and it already had begun to grow, a little.

CTA, WJF, SC 244-71.22

GRANNIES' TUG OF WAR, CENTRE ISLAND, ca. 1908. The economic boom also made life more pleasant for many early twentieth-century Toronto women who had been in the city a long time. It seems likely that not all the women involved in this tug of war could technically qualify as "grannies" in quite the sense conjured up by the photographer's title. But the picture does rather starkly suggest the last long picnic at the water's edge, especially in the more settled and established compartments of city life. It remains unclear whether this particular group of older and younger ladies was on the winning side in the Centre Island tug of war.

CTA, WJF, SC 244-196

JEWISH GIRLS AT THE TORONTO LAKEFRONT, MID- TO LATE-1900s. For the most part, the so-called "old-community" Jews of Toronto were British, prosperous, and rooted in the city since the middle of the nineteenth century. The "new-community" Jews from eastern Europe, who arrived in the late nineteenth and early twentieth centuries, were quite different. They presented some problems of adjustment for both the city at large and its more established Jewish population. It is not clear just who the "Jewish girls" identified here by the photographer are, but one might guess from their clothes and general appearance that they come from old-community families. It was the ultimately much larger and more controversial new community that would do so much to pioneer Toronto's tradition of cultural diversity in the twentieth century.

CTA, WJF, SC 244-39.22

FLOWERS IN MAY ON THE DANFORTH, ca. 1910. "The Danforth" (or Danforth Avenue — what Bloor Street is called east of the Don River) was a little like a country road at the edge of town in the early twentieth century. Robert Thomas Allen, who lived in the area during the 1920s, would later remember that in those days the "city didn't sprawl into the country ... the country came right into the city." The unnamed young woman here is obviously looking after children. They may or may not be related to her. Or, like many other women before and since, she may have found it a helpful way of making ends meet. You can *buy* flowers grown elsewhere along the Danforth today; but merely gathering them has become obsolete.

CTA, WJF, SC 244-681

DOMESTIC SCIENCE CLASS, OLD TECHNICAL SCHOOL, ca. 1910. In fact only about 57 percent of the female population in Canada was married in 1911, compared with just under 65 percent in 1951. Yet the presumed ultimate destiny for the great majority of Toronto women in the early twentieth century was still to create proper homes for men and children. The city prided itself on how seriously it took this kind of work, and "domestic" or "household" science was a frequently noted part of the local educational curriculum for girls. (A city directory of the 1920s would even boast that "TORONTO university has the only household science department of any university in the British Empire.") So-called technical education was a related local enthusiasm of the era. In 1915 the old technical school pictured here, at 149 College Street, would be superseded by the present Central Technical School at 725 Bathurst, between Harbord and Lennox streets.

CTA, WJF, SC 244-3036

MAIL-ORDER OFFICE, ROBERT SIMPSON CO., ca. 1909. Though home-making was still the presumed ultimate destiny for the great majority, even before the First World War there was already a significant enough minority of so-called "working girls" in Toronto. (In 1911 women accounted for about 13 percent of the official Canadian labour force, compared with 20 percent in 1941 and 33 percent in 1971.) For many, a full-time job was just a short stop between school and marriage. And housewives, themselves, were prominent among the customers, whose department-store mail-orders the clerks here are processing. Two of the three supervisors standing in the picture are of course men. But one (top, far right) is a Toronto woman who has at least begun to rise. She may have gone on to "work" all her life.

CTA, WJF, SC 244-136A

U OF T WOMEN'S HOCKEY TEAM, VICTORIA COLLEGE RINK, ca. 1912. The University of Toronto — already Canada's largest institution of its sort — had accepted its first women students as early as 1886. By the early 1900s, a few hundred daughters of mostly quite wealthy families were acquiring some exposure to the virtues of higher education on the U of T campus, just west of the provincial parliament buildings at Queen's Park. Emily Jennings Stowe, of Toronto, had already become the first Canadian woman authorized to practise medicine (in 1880). And the Toronto woman Clara Brett Martin had become the first Canadian female lawyer in 1895. Just before the First World War, however, the visiting British poet Rupert Brooke pronounced that, for the most part, Toronto was an "unintellectual ... well-to-do, public-school-and-varsity sort of city." These hockey-playing young ladies still seem quite steeped in this tradition.
CTA, WJF, SC 244-480

ONTARIO JOCKEY CLUB, 1913. Daughters of quite wealthy Toronto families in the early twentieth century also intermittently visited the Woodbine racetrack in the city's east end, emulating the English aristocratic passion for the "sport of kings." The annual King's Plate in May, in particular, was, among other things, a fashion show. And the women here are doing their best to make the 1913 edition a success.

CTA, WJF, 244-377

HIKERS, EGLINTON AVENUE WEST, NEAR BATHURST STREET, 1912. Another example of how "the country came right into the city" in an earlier Toronto. Eglinton Avenue today is a midtown location altogether smothered in concrete, and if you stand at the intersection of Eglinton and Bathurst, all you are likely to hear is the noise of automobiles. In 1912 the area was still what we would now call "exurban," or even rural. It seems to have been a pleasant place for energetic young women who enjoyed hiking through the city's adjacent countryside — in still rather long skirts, and boots that must have taken more than their fair share of time to get on and off.

CTA, WJF, SC 244-380

WOMEN EATING LOLLIPOPS, 1911. The quintessential daughters of Toronto's early twentieth-century age of innocence, perhaps. Only a few short years later the world would start to change forever, and Toronto women would never be quite so innocent again.

CTA, WJF, SC 244-13.43

RAINSTORM AT THE CANADIAN NATIONAL EXHIBITION, JUST AFTER THE FIRST WORLD WAR.

CTA, WJF, SC 244-25.33

2 Storm Clouds

For all types of Toronto women, two big events in the second decade of the twentieth century brought the age of innocence to a rather abrupt end. The first was the 1913 crash of the great economic boom that had begun in the late 1890s. Both the boom and its crash were Canadian variations on wider global themes. But after not much more than a decade and a half of heady growth, Torontonians were reminded that the local future had no guarantees.

As short as it was, the boom had transformed the city of the 1890s. By 1911 "Toronto proper" — already expanded geographically by recent annexations — could boast a population of close to 377,000. By birth or migration from various places, inside and outside Canada, some 168,000 new residents had arrived during the first decade of the twentieth century — a number only somewhat smaller than the city's entire population in 1891. And in 1913 it became especially clear that rapid growth of this sort could bring its own kinds of problems, especially when it all of a sudden stopped.

The second big event of the new era was announced on August 4, 1914, when King George V declared that the British empire was at war with Germany, as of 11 PM, Greenwich mean time. The Dominion of Canada was still very much a part of the empire at this point, and it was at war with Germany too (though the Canadian federal parliament in Ottawa would subsequently express its own formal approval of what the King had done). Toronto in the summer of 1914, shaped by close to a century of mass migrations from the United Kingdom — and with close to one hundred thousand residents who had been born in the United Kingdom themselves — embraced the imperial war effort without reservation.

Despite initial prophecies of a short conflict, the struggle in Europe would drag on until the fall of 1918. As the meticulous Toronto historian J.M.S. Careless has explained, some seventy thousand of the city's men "went into the forces, the weight of its younger male adult population. One in seven did not return, and of those that did, many were so badly wounded that their lives were shattered. The strains on families at home were bitter as well. Never had the city faced human loss and heartbreak on such a scale, or for so long."

REAR AT 18 WILLIAM STREET, AUGUST 28, 1914. This precisely dated photograph from the city health department was shot just over three weeks after the outbreak of the First World War. William Street (now known as St. Patrick) was just west of the early twentieth-century downtown "Ward." This was the area roughly bounded by present-day Queen, University, Gerrard, and Yonge (or at least Bay Street) — a haven of of the day for recent migrants to Toronto who did not yet have much money to spend. The quite severe economic recession that arrived in 1913 made it clear to city health officials, and others, that the heady growth of the preceding decade and a half had put considerable stress on Toronto's housing stock. The recession itself put considerable stress on the health of more than a few Toronto women as well.

CTA, Health Department Fonds (HD), RG 8-32-326

DEPARTING TORONTO SOLDIER WITH GIRL'S PICTURE IN HAT, ca. 1916. During the first year of the First World War, Canadian regulations required enlisting soldiers to present written permission from their wives or mothers. So many wives and mothers proved reluctant that the requirement was dropped in August 1915. Some women, on the other hand (as the First World War archivist Barbara Wilson has explained), "felt it was their duty to accost young men in the streets to inquire why they were not in uniform." In either case, memories of women waiting at home helped get many of the eighty-five percent of Toronto soldiers, who finally did come back from Europe, through the ordeal. As long as it lasted, one might guess a picture in your hat was moral support.

CTA, WJF, SC 244-829

CANADIAN RED CROSS AND FORD AMBULANCE, ca. 1915. Toronto women did a lot more than wait for men to come home during the First World War. One popular way of helping the war effort on the local home front was to get involved with the Red Cross. A government pamphlet of the day on Win-the-War Suggestions and Recipes urged women to "look at all the well-managed, hard working war charities — such as the Red Cross, without whose organization the agony, suffering and hideous pain and awful helplessness of millions, yes millions, would be un-assuaged, un-relieved, un-helped, and the mortality increased a hundredfold. How many of you have worked for that, as every woman should, or even given to it according to your means?"

CTA, WJF, SC 244-885

WARTIME AVIATION IN TORONTO, ca. 1916. In Toronto, as elsewhere, more than a few women took up jobs vacated by men, who went overseas during the First World War. Banks and shipping departments of express offices were among the first new employers (though a few bank spokesmen predictably expressed "reservations about the capabilities of female employees"). Many local manufacturers were initially quite reluctant. But by 1916 there was a critical labour shortage and attitudes quickly changed. The women here are binding copper strips around the edges of airplane wings. All told, Canadian Aeroplanes Ltd., of Toronto, would produce some twelve hundred training planes for the Royal Air Force in the UK, and thirty "Felixstowe" flying boats for the United States.

CTA, WJF, SC 244-4554

LAST PAY, MUNITIONS WORKERS, SOUTHEAST CORNER OF KING AND DUFFERIN STREETS, 1918. The most sought-after jobs for many female war workers were in munitions plants. As archivist Barbara Wilson has explained: "Women had heard of the vast sums of money to be made in munitions work and wanted a share." The first employees of this sort in Canada started on the job in the fall of 1916. Munitions manufacturers "found to their surprise and delight that women were indeed capable, especially in the intricate task of fuse assembling." Judging by the looks on their faces, some of the women waiting for their last pay in 1918 here had mixed emotions when the war finally came to and end.

CTA, WJF, SC 244-924

BABY CLINIC AT ST. CHRISTOPHER HOUSE, FIRST WORLD WAR. In some ways the war improved the local economy, but in others the 1913 recession lived on. Just before the recession started in earnest, government research had already shown that parts of Toronto had the same alarmingly high rates of infant mortality as some notorious parts of London and New York. Local statistics indicated that as many as 131 out of every 1,000 live babies were dying before they were a year old. When the war broke out in Europe, the city health department was organizing a new local "Division of Child Hygiene." St. Christopher House had been established by the Presbyterian Church in Canada at 67 Bellevue Place — or what is now called Wales Avenue, just northeast of Bathurst and Dundas. And it was one of several Toronto locations where "baby clinics" were held to help stop what one study called "the slaughter of the innocents."

CTA, HD, RG 8-32-334

ARMISTICE DAY IN TORONTO, NOVEMBER 11, 1918. If some of these people look a little tired, it's probably because they are. The first news of the end of the First World War reached Toronto over the Associated Press wires to local newspapers at 2:55 on the morning of November 11. According to a report in the *Globe* newspaper of the day: "Within a few minutes many whistles in all parts of the city were blowing full blast." A little after 3 AM "a procession, mostly of women munition workers, paraded Yonge Street, cheering, wildly beating tin pans and blowing whistles. By this time a crowd began to gather all along Yonge Street." Alas, a few Toronto women had one last role to play in the war effort, and could not join the celebrations right away. Female operators of telephone exchanges were swamped with calls from other parts of Ontario. As the *Globe* reporter put it: "The girls worked heroically without any let up to help give the wonderful tidings to all parts of the waiting, anxious but sleeping Province."

CTA, WJF, SC 244-888

BILL NIX RETURNS FROM THE GREAT WAR IN EUROPE, 1919. After the armistice celebrations calmed down, more than a few Toronto women were reminded of just how much grief the First World War had brought to their lives. Some ten thousand Torontonians had died (in a city that still had not many more than half a million people). A great many of the sixty thousand enlisted men who did return were physically and/or emotionally wounded, in one sense or another. And tales of appallingly mutilated Great War veterans in such places as Christie Street Hospital (no doubt somewhat embroidered) would form part of the mental furniture for young people who grew up in Toronto in the 1920s and 1930s. Mr. Nix here is at least walking more or less under his own steam, and can still make some women happy. The lady immediately to his right, however (his mother, perhaps), seems to have begun to grasp the unhappier side of the war for him.

CTA, WJF, SC 244-904A

WAR WIDOWS, ca. 1920. For some time after it was all over, official Toronto continued to pay its respects to those women who had suffered most from the Great War in Europe. And the Canadian federal government in Ottawa provided the widows of fallen soldiers with pensions (though they were cancelled if the recipients remarried). In the end, as the Toronto historian J.M.S. Careless has put it, "There was pride no less than mourning" in the city, "and perhaps the assurance of having come through a cruel testing." In 1918 an editorial in the Toronto *Globe* had also pointed out that: "Certainly during this period of testing the Canadian women have developed a capacity for leadership and for organization which has set the pace for the men." As the ladies pictured here suggest, some among the Canadian women would have to develop a new capacity for bearing grief as well.

CTA, WJF, SC 244-12.18

LITTLE MOTHERS' CLASS, ST. HELEN'S SEPARATE SCHOOL, OCTOBER 31, 1919. The war itself ended in 1918, but in a number of respects the other Toronto unhappiness, crystallized by the recession of 1913, would hang on into the earlier 1920s. And economic hard times continued to help focus attention on the city's early twentieth-century problems with infant mortality. Here, about a year after the end of the Great War, older Toronto schoolgirls are given classroom instruction in the arts and crafts of caring for infant children. St. Helen's Separate School was part of Ontario's partly publicly funded system of Catholic education (dating from the exotic mid-nineteenth-century era, when Ontario and Quebec had been a single "United Province of Canada"). Adherents of the Roman Catholic Church accounted for just over 12 percent of the city of Toronto population in 1921. The proportion would subsequently rise steadily, all the way to almost 39 percent in 1971, before coming to rest at 34 percent in 1991.

CTA, HD, RG 8-32-611

NUDE MODEL AT ONTARIO SCHOOL OF ART, THE GRANGE, CA. 1920.
CTA, WJF, SC 244-80.28

3 Anything Goes

In Toronto, as in other places, the First World War opened a lot of closed doors. To start with, the capacity for leadership and organization shown by women at war at last convinced male politicians to give women at peace the right to vote in Canadian federal and provincial elections. And this may have helped prompt another innovation. In the great turmoil that descended upon many parts of the world in the wake of the Great War, E.C. Drury's Farmer-Labour coalition (1919–1923) became the first third-party government to stalk the corridors of power in Canada's most populous province.

In the broadest sweep of the twentieth century in the city, Drury and his Farmer-Labourers were a kind of early rehearsal for Bob Rae and the New Democrats, some seventy years later. And the Drury regime was also soon followed by an aggressive turn in another direction. In 1923 Queen's Park at Toronto fell into the hands of born-again Conservatives, led by G. Howard Ferguson. "Fergie's" platform, a journalist of the day explained, was to revive "the old-time political religion" and "give the boys some political jazz."

The First World War had prompted some other experiments in closing open doors as well. The prohibition of the sale of alcoholic beverages, a somewhat jocular version of which prevailed throughout Ontario from 1916 to 1927, is probably the best example. The Drury government had ardently supported and even strengthened what was officially known as the Ontario Temperance Act. In the provincial capital city, Fergie managed to bring an earlier "Tory Toronto" back to life, partly by promising to get rid of "the OTA." Almost four years after he was first elected, the promise was fulfilled.

Meanwhile, in the last half of the 1920s, Toronto became reacquainted with its earlier great economic boom. The return of the old-time political religion took a certain toll. But in other respects the spirit of innovation hung on. "Toronto proper" had grown from some 377,000 people in 1911 to 522,000 in 1921. It would rise again to 631,000 in 1931. By 1931 the main thrust of growth had already shifted to the city proper's adjacent suburbs. Federal statisticians reported that some 818,000 people were living in the "greater Toronto" of the day. The real twentieth century in the city pushed off the lid of the box it was still inside, and more than a few Toronto women became more daring. The earlier age of innocence would never be retrieved.

CABINET MINISTERS' WIVES, ONTARIO FARMER-LABOUR GOVERNMENT, ca. 1920. The United Farmers of Ontario accounted for forty-five of the fifty-six supporters of Drury's Farmer-Labour government in the provincial legislature. Unlike Bob Rae and the New Democrats some seventy years later, the Drury government had a pronounced rural-progressive tilt. The family farm was still a driving force in the regional economy. But the "Canadian-American" industrial revolution in Ontario (US branch plant and otherwise) had already begun to eclipse the old agricultural dominance. The provincial capital city gave only one of its ten seats to a Farmer-Labour supporter in the 1919 election — in the east-end riding of Riverdale. For its main part in the short-lived revolution, the fabled "Tory Toronto" of the day sent five Liberals and a mere four Conservatives to Queen's Park.

CTA, WJF, SC 244-8053

MISS JENNIE BROWN, RUNNYMEDE AREA, JULY 1923. Even apart from the wives of the Drury cabinet ministers (who had just left Queen's Park by late July 1923), Toronto still had its own rural-progressive tilt in the 1920s. "A familiar picture presented to residents of Runnymede," a *Globe* reporter noted when this John Boyd photograph appeared in the newspaper, "is that of a herd of cattle grazing on the grassy slopes at Evelyn Crescent and Glendonwynne Road."
CTA, G&M, SC 266-11686

THE DATTEN FAMILY'S NEW BUNGALOW, SILVERTHORN, 1921. In 1921 the north end of Silverthorn Avenue was actually in what was then called York township, rather than the city proper. But in both the city and its suburbs, the ultimate aspiration for the majority of Toronto women after the First World War was still to be the mistress of a family with a home of its own — the urban successor, as it were, to the old family farm. In the new age of innovation, at least some parts of the Toronto real-estate industry tried to help make the dream come true at less cost. According to an adjacent sign that does not appear in the photograph, "This bungalow built in a day by A.E. LePage." The price was $2,975. By way of comparison, in 1920 a female school teacher in Toronto earned from $1,000 to $2,000 per year. A male teacher, who on the assumptions of the day typically had to support a wife and family, earned from $1,625 to $2,500.

CTA, WJF, SC 244-31.43

KEW BEACH PADDLERS, 1922. Even in the changing 1920s, there were still Toronto women who kept much older memories alive — back way beyond the family farm and even the town of York to the more ancient days of the fur trade in Canada and, back still further, even to the age of the primeval Iroquoian forest, when everyone in Toronto paddled a canoe. In the era after the First World War, Kew Beach (echoing a name from another native land) was in the east end of the city, also home to such organizations as the Balmy Beach Canoe Club and the Don Canoe Club. The Argonaut Rowing Club, the Parkdale Canoe Club, and the Toronto Canoe Club graced the west end.

CTA, WJF, SC 244-57.21

MARY PICKFORD AND DOUGLAS FAIRBANKS ON A TORONTO VISIT, MARCH 1924. The quite remarkable Mary Pickford had begun her life as Gladys Smith in 1892, in a now long-since-vanished house on University Avenue in Toronto, between Gerrard and Elm streets. Two events that took place when she was a mere five years old shaped the rest of her life: the death of her father, and her first appearance on stage, at the old Princess Theatre. She was an authentic child prodigy, and it quickly became clear that her talent could help support her mother, brother, and sister. A few years later, she began touring Canada and the United States as "Baby Gladys." When she was fourteen, she talked her way into a starring role in a Broadway play by David Belasco, who rechristened her Mary Pickford. Two years later, she talked D.W. Griffith into giving her a start on a dazzling career as "America's sweetheart" in early Hollywood movies. In 1919, some five years before John Boyd took the photograph here, she had formed the United Artists Corporation, with Griffith, Charlie Chaplin, and Douglas Fairbanks (whom she subsequently married). It seems that she never quite forgot her short childhood in Toronto. In the 1960s she would tell the journalist Clyde Gilmour, over the telephone: "Last night I had a dream about Toronto ... And, as usual in my dreams I was a little girl again. A little girl in Toronto with long golden curls."

CTA, G&M, SC 266-2234-G

MRS. AMBROSE SMALL, WILL CASE, APRIL 28, 1924. Theresa or "Mrs. Ambrose" Small lacked Mary Pickford's prodigious talent. But she, too, was a local celebrity of sorts in Toronto after the First World War. Her husband, Ambrose Small, had owned what the press called "vast theatrical holdings" in various parts of Canada. Late in 1919 — the same year that Mary Pickford and her colleagues formed United Artists — Small sold his theatres and vanished without a trace. On December 2 he had lunched with his wife downtown, and then met with his lawyer to wrap up the theatrical deal in the afternoon. Neither Theresa, his lawyer, nor a great many other curious people ever saw him again. The resulting official police investigation, which would remain active until 1960, remains unsolved to this day. Suspicions of kidnapping or murder could never be proved. And in his 1987 Toronto novel, *In the Skin of a Lion*, Michael Ondaatje speculated that Small eventually took up a secret new life with another woman. Whatever really happened, the problem of what to do with Ambrose Small's fortune, which remained intact long after his disappearance, was a boon to city lawyers. In this photograph, John Boyd has captured Theresa Small on her way to the will case of April 1924, where she fought with her in-laws over control of the estate. She would leave the courtroom in charge of the lion's share of the funds at stake (some $2.5 million), and "without any stain, whatsoever, upon her character."

CTA, G&M, SC 266-2482-S

YOUNG LADIES JUDGING DOMESTIC SCIENCE, CANADIAN NATIONAL EXHIBITION, SEPTEMBER 9, 1925. Even in an era of innovation, the mistresses of Toronto homes were still expected to manage them with due attention to the precepts of domestic science. And enthusiasm for the subject was not confined to what we know as inner Toronto in the late twentieth century. Here (left to right), Misses Helen Cuttle and Rose Robinson from York county, and Dorothy Pallett, Verna Nurse, and Pearl Church from Peel county (all in the then quite rural "905" part of the Greater Toronto Area today) have come downtown to the CNE to judge "home cooking, sewing, manufactured garments and other things applicable to the home." The city's annual late-summer industrial exhibition, which traced its official history back to 1878, had rechristened itself the Canadian National Exhibition in 1912. The new name was a sign of Canada's second most-populous city's expanding ambitions, at the height of the early twentieth-century boom. But despite its "increasingly industrial aspect," the *Globe* report accompanying this photograph stressed, the CNE "has never lost touch with the basic industry of Canada. Agricultural displays have increased from year to year."

CTA, G&M, SC 266-6230

JAMAICAN WEDDING, JULY 29, 1926. The great migration from the old British West Indies in the Caribbean Sea, which has made such a contribution to late twentieth-century Toronto, would not get seriously under way until the 1960s. As with so much else, however, there were modest earlier rehearsals after the First World War. At what the newspaper called "one of the most elaborate weddings that have taken place among members of the local Jamaican colony" here, we know that the bride is Rachel Adina Stephenson and the groom is Joshua Michael Williams. To the right of the bride are (left to right): Agnes Brown, Doris Bailey, and Francie Gibbons. The wedding took place at the British Methodist Episcopal Church on Chestnut Street. A reception was held at 553 Queen Street West.

CTA, G&M, SC 266-8380-S

GRECIAN DANCERS: MISSES AILEEN PARKER AND PHYLLIS STRATHY IN CONSERVATORY FOUNTAIN, AUGUST 24, 1925. Exactly how John Boyd came up with this photograph, and exactly where the "conservatory fountain" is located remains unclear (though it may be the old Graphic Arts Building at the CNE). Among other things, it seems to say a lot about how some young women had become more daring by the late summer of 1925.

CTA, G&M, SC 266-6044-G

MISS ALDEANE EAGAN, SKI CLUB MASQUERADE, APRIL 16, 1926. Oddly enough, this photograph from a party at the Toronto Ski Club is one of the few pictures in our collection which alludes to the plain fact that there is typically some snow in Toronto for certain parts of the year (less than in Montreal, but a little more than in New York City). By the spring of 1926, in any case, even the headlines in Toronto newspapers were pronouncing that the great boom of the earlier twentieth century had returned at last.

CTA, G&M, SC 266-7579

KENSINGTON MARKET, JULY 15, 1926 (above). According to the *Globe* of the day, this was a scene "typical of the Jewish market on Kensington Avenue north of Dundas, where every Thursday there gather vendors of wares of almost every imaginable sort, from live fowl to dress goods." By the end of the First World War, the new-community Jews of Toronto from eastern Europe were well-settled into their pioneering of the neighbourhood west and northwest of the old downtown Ward, as a historic reception area for new migrants to the city. What they pioneered would subsequently fall into the hands of successive new migrant communities, especially as the later twentieth century progressed. But in the 1920s, Jewish was the single-largest ethnic origin in Toronto after British, by some considerable margin. In 1931 some 7.2 percent of the city of Toronto population reported its ethnic origin as Jewish — up from 6.6 percent in 1921, 4.9 percent in 1911, and 1.5 percent in 1901.

CTA, G&M, SC 266-8245-G

CHINESE CELEBRATION, MISS MARY LEE, TORONTO, OCTOBER 18, 1928 (opposite). In the very late twentieth century, the dominant mood on the south Spadina strip, off which Kensington Market is a kind of annex, is "Chinese culture." Though a much more recent Toronto development on its present scale, this too had its modest earlier rehearsals. Here, on behalf of the Eastern Canada Section of the Kuomintang in Canada, Mary Lee of Toronto is presenting flowers to the wife of the visiting "special envoy from the National Government of China to the United States." At the time, Mary Lee was a quite rare Toronto woman of her particular old-world descent. In 1921 there were 1,947 Chinese males and and a mere 88 Chinese females in the city. And this early "bachelor society" would be artificially and arbitrarily perpetuated by the Canadian federal government's Chinese Immigration Act of 1923 (which, for most practical purposes, proscribed further Chinese immigration to Canada, until it was rescinded in 1947). Chinese laundries and restaurants were nonetheless widely dispersed throughout the city in the 1920s, 1930s, and earlier 1940s. Ernest Hemingway, who lived in Toronto for two brief periods after the First World War, once wrote to his friend Gertrude Stein in Paris that "contrary to my remembrance the cuisine here is good," especially at some "Chinese places."

CTA, G&M, SC 266-15256

OF CHINA
IN CANADA
EASTERN SECTION
CONVENTION

WILLARD HALL, TORONTO, WOMEN'S CHRISTIAN TEMPERANCE UNION, JUNE 17, 1929. The local Toronto District branch of the WCTU had lost a battle when the Ontario provincial government finally replaced prohibition with a government-controlled system of marketing alcoholic beverages, in the spring of 1927. But the war against the "demon rum" in the wider global village carried on. This photograph was taken at a 1929 meeting that laid plans for a WCTU World Convention, held in Toronto in 1931. Strictly speaking, only Mrs. F.C. Ward, Toronto District president (third from left), qualifies as a Toronto woman. The other three ladies are her guests (from left to right): Miss Sui Kanamori, an early feminist leader from Tokyo; Dr. Anna Adams Gordon, WCTU World President (from Evanstown, Illinois), and (to the right of Mrs. Ward) Mrs. Gordon Wright, WCTU Dominion of Canada President (from London, Ontario, and well-known in her day as a daring public speaker).

CTA, G&M, SC 266-16975

WOMEN'S OLYMPIC TEAM LEAVES UNION STATION, MAY 1928. Even with its damaged glass negative, this photograph captures the uniquely buoyant spirit of innovation that marked the lives of many Toronto women in the last few years of the 1920s, just before the sudden shock of the Great Crash in October 1929. These particular members of the first women's team to compete for Canada in the Olympics are bound for the 1928 summer games at Amsterdam. They are (from left to right): Myrtle Cook, Jean Thompson, Ethel Smith, Florence Bell, Ethel Catherwood, Fannie Rosenfeld, Miss A.E.M. Parkes (chaperone), and Dorothy Prior. All are from Toronto, except for Jean Thompson (from Penetang, Ontario, due north). Florence Bell, Ethel Catherwood, Myrtle Cook, Fannie Rosenfeld, and Ethel Smith would all go on to win gold medals for Canada. They had probably been encouraged by the home-town send-off from "500 sports fans" at Union Station.

CTA, G&M, SC 266-20610

SALLY LEE ORCHESTRA, CONCERT AT CHRISTIE STREET HOSPITAL, JANUARY 21, 193[illegible]

4 And the Band Played On

The folk wisdom is that when New York catches a cold, Toronto comes down with pneumonia. But gold-mining on the Canadian Shield in northern Ontario helped some parts of the province's capital city weather the Great Depression of the 1930s better than in other places (including Canada's largest big city of the day in Montreal). In 1934 the old Standard Mining Exchange and the old Toronto Stock Exchange joined forces as the new Toronto Stock Exchange — the third-largest enterprise of its sort in all of North America.

The fabled Great Crash in the fall of 1929, nonetheless, did resound with a loud and unjoyful noise in Toronto. By May 1932, the Dominion Bureau of Statistics index of Canadian stock prices had fallen to 38.6, from a high of 235.4 just before the wild panic set in, late in October 1929. General Motors of Canada, in nearby Oshawa, had produced 104,198 passenger cars and trucks in 1929. In 1932 it produced a mere 19,565. Almost a third of all the jobs in Toronto in 1929 had disappeared by 1933. And it has been estimated that in early 1935, about one-quarter of the population in Toronto and its suburbs was dependent on public relief.

All this brought great new grief and hard times to more than a few women in the city. Yet the big economic picture gradually became not quite so depressingly dismal after 1933. Nowadays, we know that, even at certain points in the much more recent downsizing decade of the 1990s, unemployment in various parts of Canada has once again been as high as it was in at least the later parts of the mythical Dirty Thirties.

Photographs of Toronto women in the era inevitably reflect the new grief and hardship — and the accompanying political and social turbulence as well. But they also reflect something else. Even people who were hit hard by the economic dislocation had to get on with their lives, and in most cases they did. The great majority of the Toronto labour force remained employed, even at the height of the depression in the earlier 1930s. The cost of living fell, along with employment levels and the stock market. And in many different ways, the new music of the jazz age, which had begun to change life in a lot of big cities after the First World War, just played on, and on, and on.

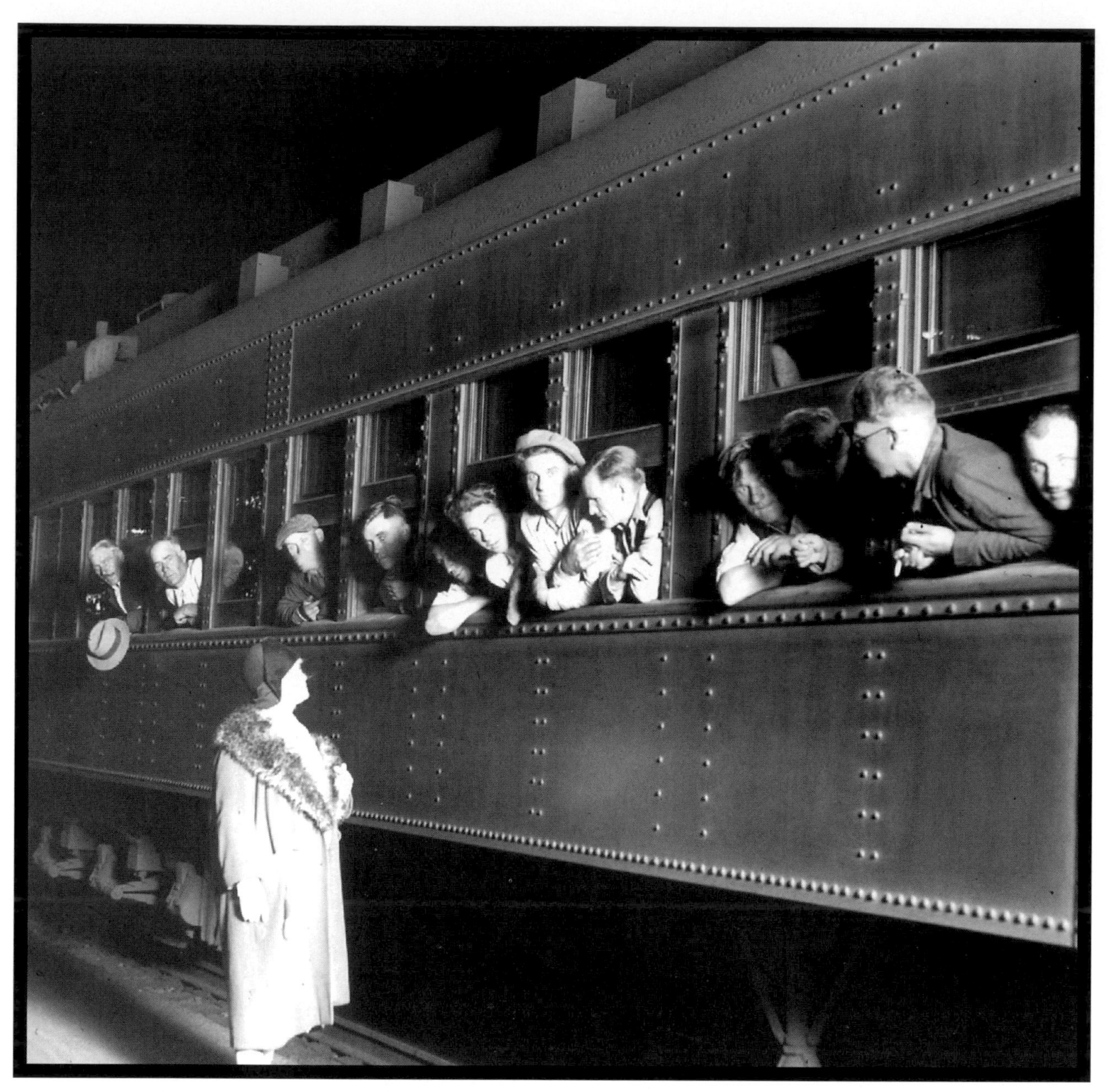

SAYING GOODBYE TO UNEMPLOYED TORONTO MEN, LEAVING FOR THE NORTH, OCTOBER 1, 1931. To help cope with the grim winters of 1930–31, 1931–32, and 1932–33, the Ontario government established "jobless camps" along the lines of the province's northern railways. The unemployed men here are part of a group of two hundred who had been sleeping in the Don valley. They are bound for the Kenora area, to work on "the projected Trans Canada highway." Bidding "her boys goodbye" (as the newspaper put it) is Mrs. J. Sutherland, "an active worker among the unemployed."

CTA, G&M, SC 266-25474

LADY EATON AND TWO DAUGHTERS AT HUNT CLUB MEET, ca. 1930. By the time the Great Crash had begun to wreak its destruction, the former Flora McCrea, a nurse from Omemee, Ontario, was well-established as "Lady Eaton"– dowager queen of the increasingly Canada-wide Eaton's department store empire that was anchored in Toronto. Her husband, Sir John Craig Eaton (son of founder, Timothy, and knighted in 1915 as a reward for outfitting a unit known as the Eaton Machine Gun Battery in the First World War), had been dead since 1922. Her son, John David Eaton, was not yet old enough to preside over the business. (For the time being, Timothy's nephew, R.Y. Eaton, served as regent.) Quite a few Toronto women and men of the day worked at Eaton's. Some sources say it was a "sweatshop" which did not pay particularly well. The point stressed in others is that it was loyal to its employees: a job at Eaton's was a ticket to surviving the Great Depression. Much more recently, alas, Eaton's itself has been struggling with hard times.
CTA, WJF, SC 244-1601

FLOWER SELLERS AT ITALIAN PICNIC, AUGUST 1, 1932. Even the depths of the Great Depression were not enough to stop the annual picnic of Toronto's "Italian Colony," which was being held by this point at the CNE grandstand. By the early 1930s, Italian had already become the city of Toronto's third-largest reported ethnic origin — after British and Jewish. (And there are some incidental Italian characters in Morley Callaghan's first Toronto novel of 1928, *Strange Fugitive.*) But people reporting Italian origins still accounted for only 2.1 percent of the city's total population in 1931. The proportion would rise to no more than 2.7 percent in 1951, on the eve of the great migrations that would more than quadruple the Italian community's relative importance in the city, in a single decade. The Toronto woman on the left here, in 1932, is Louise Racioppo, and her flower-selling companion on the right is Dora Mably. (Dora is a common Italian first name. "Mably," on the other hand, seems to suggest that Toronto's long twentieth-century tradition of inter-cultural romance had put down some deep enough roots by the 1930s as well.)

CTA, G&M, SC 266-27671

MAY DAY PARADE, RIVERDALE PARK, MAY 1, 1935. Based on unemployment statistics, the Depression in Canada peaked economically in 1933. But in Toronto, as in some other places, the political peak came in 1935. The demagogic Mitch Hepburn's Ontario Liberals had ejected the Tories from Queen's Park in June 1934. And on January 1, 1935, the local body politic elected the labour activist, Jimmie Simpson, sometimes called Toronto's first CCF Mayor (the Co-operative Commonwealth Federation being the ancestor of the present-day New Democrats). The city women depicted here at Riverdale Park are, in fact, just marshalling for a longer march. They would ultimately be part of what the newspaper headlines described as the "10,000 Radicals" who gathered on May 1, 1935, to hear "a blazing barrage of radical oratory" from "the new bandshell at Queen's Park." The *Globe* noted that "workers have increased greatly in class-consciousness and political influence in recent years." It also stressed, however, how "Good humour mingles with Socialism as Orderly throng Gathers in Queen's Park — Police Present Only to Regulate Traffic."

CTA, G&M, SC 266-36526

PUPILS ON RELIEF STRIKE, DANFORTH PARK SCHOOL, EAST YORK, NOVEMBER 12, 1935 (above). The peak of the Depression, political and economic, was especially hard on what was then known as the township of East York. According to the urban historian, James Lemon, in the mid-1930s "in East York 45 per cent of the population was on the dole and working residents paid much of the cost." The *Globe* article accompanying this particular photograph, from November 1935, noted that "several schools in East York township were 'picketed' yesterday by children of many families receiving relief, in an effort to gain support for the 'cash relief' demands." The picture shows "some of the placard decorated children who tried, unsuccessfully in most cases, to induce their young friends to stay away from school."

CTA, G&M, SC 266-38454

OPENING DAY AT THE CLUB ESQUIRE, LAKESHORE ROAD AT PARKSIDE DRIVE, NOVEMBER 26, 1936 (opposite). By late 1936, the local economy had improved enough to attract a new nightclub near the waterfront in the west end, complete with "dinner (inc. dancing show)" for $1.25. The dancing show boasted "25 gorgeous gals, complete cast of 36." Pictured here (left to right) are Doris Carroll, Rita Mackie, and Connie Constant. Sensibly enough, from various economic points of view, the photograph was actually taken the day before the Club Esquire opened on November 27.

CTA, G&M, SC 266-42039

LADY GODIVA AND HER HORSE, PEEPING TOM, "RIDE OF THE AGES," CANADIAN NATIONAL EXHIBITION, SEPTEMBER 3, 1935. There had been some lively entertainment in Toronto even at the political peak of the Great Depression. Alas, the name of the young lady, who is rather demurely impersonating Lady Godiva here, is unknown.

CTA, G&M, SC 266-37746

JUNIOR LEAGUE CABARET, MARCH 6, 1937. The "Junior League Flower Show and Nightclub," held upstairs at the still quite new Eaton's College Street store, was judged by some Toronto women as "the highlight of the season's social activities" in 1937. The show went on for five days, and there were cabarets featuring entertainment by Junior League members in both the Round Room and the Auditorium. The entertainers here are (left to right): Mrs. J.M. McAvity, Kay Laidlaw, and Mrs. David Cassels. Mrs. Margaret Eaton was "chairman of committee in charge."

CTA, G&M, SC 266-43558

WOMAN SMOKING CIGAR, FEBRUARY 16, 1937. Again, the name of this sophisticated lady — nail-polished, in a satin dress, and reading last month's issue of Movie Mirror (which cost all of ten cents) — remains a mystery. There are reasons to believe that she is a relative of John Boyd's, and she may bear some resemblance to his sister, Lillian, whom he had photographed perched on the roof of a car a little more than eight years before. (But if this is true, why did he just write "Woman smoking cigar" in his logbook?) Whoever she is, she seems to be saying that the daring ways some Toronto women picked up after the First World War are still in style.

CTA, G&M, SC 266-43266

TORONTO INDIAN COUNCIL CLUB, MARCH 12, 1938. The *Globe* article, for which this photograph was taken, began rather poetically: "An Indian drum throbbed in the moonlight on the banks of the Humber Saturday night and Indians in full ceremonial dress and feathers silently moved to take their places in the Council of the Crow or Warm Moon, annual ceremony of the Toronto Indian Council Club." According to John Boyd's logbook, the women in this case are (left to right): Ivy Maison, Mrs. J.J. Sussmuth, Mrs. Grey Owl, Ruth McFarlane, and Mignon Sussmuth. The woman Boyd identifies as Mrs. Grey Owl may be one of the aboriginal wives of the gentle fraud, Archie Belaney, who pretended he was Grey Owl for the reading public in Canada, and especially the United Kingdom (though it is not easy to see a resemblance with other published photographs). From the standpoint of the late twentieth century, there are a number of things wrong with what is depicted here. But it may also suggest a few other things we have subsequently lost, and ought to try to find again.

CTA, G&M, SC 266-50111

MAY "BILLIE" HALLAM, MISS TORONTO 1937, JULY 18, 1937. The somewhat improving economy of 1937 helped prompt "the first city-wide" Miss Toronto contest "held in eleven years." It was sponsored by the city police department, and attracted 360 contestants. The winner, Billie Hallam, was "a seventeen-year-old student and softball pitcher," who lived on Booth Avenue in the east end. She was "a tall slim brunette, straight as a sapling with a flashing smile and natural dignity." The 1937 contest was "such a success" that it was "declared it would be an annual event."
CTA, G&M, SC 266-45820

NAN MORRIS, MISS TORONTO 1939, AND HER MOTHER, JULY 9, 1939. "A few days ago," the *Globe* reported, "she was merely an attractive salesgirl behind a notions counter in a large department store ... Today she's the most talked-about girl in Toronto." Referring to the three-hundred-dollar cash prize, Nan Morris herself said "I've never had so much money in my life." Nan ("who has a kind heart, a courtly carriage and comely figure") had come to Toronto with her family from London, England, when she was seven years old, and the family lived in "a modest home" on Yorkville Avenue. Nan's "brother Harry entered her application" in the contest "without her knowledge."

CTA, G&M, SC 266-59666

RACIST SIGNS AT FALLINGBROOK BEACH, JUNE 27, 1938. The height of the Great Depression in 1933 had helped bring Adolf Hitler to power in Germany. His blatant legitimization of anti-semitism across the ocean gave Toronto's Jewish community, which had grown from a mere 1.5 percent of the city's population in 1901 to 7.2 percent in 1931, some grounds for concern. These two young women, on the waterfront in what was then Scarborough township, just east of the Toronto city limits, are showing a side of the local scene that stiffened the concern. After a six-hour riot between Jewish and non-Jewish youths in the west-end Christie Pits, some five years before this photograph was taken, a broad-minded Jewish shopkeeper had told the *Daily Star* that the majority of "people here are too broad-minded" to stoop to racist politics. As in other parts of the world, however, there was anti-semitism in Toronto, as well as in Frankfurt or Berlin.

CTA, G&M, SC 266-52350

WOMEN'S AUXILIARY, OLD MOUNT SINAI HOSPITAL, ca. 1939. In the broader-minded city itself, Toronto's new-community Jews from eastern Europe had become quite established by the late 1930s. "Old" Mount Sinai Hospital was founded as a kosher medical institution in 1922, at 100 Yorkville Avenue. (The name was borrowed from the hospital in New York — a big city that has particularly inspired both the Jews of Toronto and Toronto at large. "New" Mount Sinai Hospital in Toronto was established on University Avenue in 1953.) By the late 1920s, Jewish activism in both local and provincial politics had persuaded the Ontario government to lend Old Mount Sinai a helping hand. But even on the eve of the Second World War, the Women's Auxiliary was still playing a crucial role in the hospital's success. Dorothy Goldstick Dworkin (seated in the second row at the left, with a floral collar, and without a hat) had been in charge of the group from the start, and had earlier operated a free Jewish dispensary in the old Ward.

Multicultural History Society of Ontario, Photographic Collection (MHSO/PC)

HOME-FRONT GLAMOUR GIRL AND HOOPS, KIWANIS KARNIVAL, CASA LOMA, SEPTEMBER 2, 1942.

CTA, G&M, SC 266-81117

5 What a Lovely War

Of course a real war is never lovely at all. And thousands of Toronto men would once again make the supreme sacrifice in the new great international conflict that finally ended the Great Depression. Yet in all of Canada, some lessons had been learned from the wrenching experience of 1914–1918. Fate and the active decisions of various Canadians would conspire to make "World War II" in Toronto a more benign and constructive global event.

To start with, Canada itself was no longer automatically at war when a British ultimatum about German troops in Poland expired, on September 3, 1939. In Toronto and such places as Halifax, Winnipeg, and Vancouver, ties to what was now more commonly known as the "British Empire and Commonwealth" still ran deep enough. No one doubted that Canada would fight. But the federal government in Ottawa took care to consult its elected parliament, before making its own declaration of war on September 10.

Then Prime Minister William Lyon Mackenzie King — grandson of the leader of the Upper Canadian Rebellion of 1837 (*and* the first mayor of the new city of Toronto in 1834) — managed to kill quite a lot of time promising "conscription if necessary but not necessarily conscription." In 1939–1945 raw Canadian recruits were not as lightly sent into danger as they had been in 1914–1918 in Europe and other faraway parts of the world. All told, there had been more than 68,000 Canadian casualties in the First World War. In the Second World War, there would be less than 47,000.

"Toronto and its suburbs," home to almost 910,000 people in 1941, was increasingly looking beyond Ontario's provincial borders to the country at large, and it followed the Canada-wide trends. World War II brought less grief to the city than World War I. And it *did* bring the Great Depression to a sudden halt. (The Canada-wide unemployment rate dropped from 11.4 percent in 1939 to 4.4 percent in 1941 and 1.7 percent in 1943.) As war historians W.A.B. Douglas and Brereton Greenhous have explained, in "1939 Canada had been wracked by the Depression." In 1945 "it was booming" and "incredibly ... had become a power in the world, with the third largest navy, the fourth-largest air force, and an army of almost seven divisions." It probably ought not to be surprising that, even with the unavoidable horror of war, more than a few Toronto women in the first half of the 1940s also seem to have had a lovely time.

MONA PARKER AT LATHE, INGLIS PLANT, AUGUST 24, 1940. To help win the Second World War, Ms. Parker and other Toronto women made Bren guns at revived facilities of the old John Inglis Company on Strachan Avenue, in the industrial west end. When the war was over Inglis had made, among many other things, some 186,000 Bren guns. It had also become the largest arms manufacturer in all of the "Empire and Commonwealth" (including the United Kingdom itself).

CTA, G&M, SC 266-68286

WOMEN IN THE ROYAL CANADIAN AIR FORCE, WAR LOAN PARADE, SEPTEMBER 10, 1940. In fact, what was at first called the Canadian Women's Auxiliary Air Force (later the Women's Division, RCAF) was not formally organized until some ten months after this photograph was taken. These two ladies — Mrs. D'Arcy Greig (left) and Mrs. Richard Gething — are perhaps associated with Kathleen O. Walker of the Ottawa Red Cross Motor Transport Corps, who eventually became the RCAF women's division's first senior officer. The division's training depot would soon enough be located on Jarvis Street in Toronto. Its motto was: "They serve that men may fly."

CTA, G&M, SC 266-68807

MOUNT PLEASANT BEAUTY, MAY 22, 1940. German forces had captured Amiens and Arras in France, the day before this photograph was taken. But the struggle to become Miss Toronto 1940 was still in progress back home. Though this young lady ("Mount Pleasant Beauty" in the photographer's log) appeared in the North Toronto district semi-finals, she did not go on to compete in the final city-wide contest. John Boyd, nonetheless, took several pictures of her, and if it had been up to him she probably would have won.

CTA, G&M, SC 266-66221

CIGARETTE GIRLS, ROYAL REGIMENT DANCE, OCTOBER 3, 1941. According to the copy in the *Globe*, the proper name for the function involved here was the Red and Blue Carnival. And it was held "at Columbus Hall under the auspices of the Women's Auxiliary of the Royal Regiment of Canada." The two "tray sellers" are Miss Ruth Wythe (left) and Mrs. Gordon McKnight.

CTA, G&M, SC 266-763705

THREE WOMEN, TAKING ADVANTAGE OF THE GREAT OUTDOORS, LATE SPRING, 1940 (above). The names of the three ladies are (left to right): Verna Screeve, Rella Aylestock, and Phyllis Hooper. The street is Borden Avenue on an early Sunday afternoon. Ms. Aylestock has just dropped in on her two friends, after attending the services of the African Methodist Episcopal Church on Soho Street. She had come to Toronto from Listowel, Ontario, the year before, to join her sisters who were already living in the city. Verna Screeve and Phyllis Hooper are cousins. Ms. Hooper's mother had come to Toronto much earlier, from the North Buxton area in southwestern Ontario.

Rella Braithwaite, Private Collection

THREE WOMEN, TAKING ADVANTAGE OF THE GREAT OUTDOORS, MARCH 23, 1941 (opposite). All that is really known about this photograph are the names of the three ladies (from left to right): Doris Shaw, Rose Burkett, and Jeanne Tuniff. One might speculate about the street from the houses and so forth, but the location is not made clear in the local sources. The picture was taken in the very early spring of 1941, some four days after what a standard global chronology describes as "German air raids on London resumed."

CTA, G&M, SC 266-72593

AGNES MACPHAIL WHISPERS IN MITCH HEPBURN'S EAR, JUNE 19, 1941. In the *Canadian Encyclopedia* of the 1980s, Naomi Black describes Agnes Macphail as "the only woman elected to Canada's Parliament in 1921, the first federal election in which women had the vote." Ms. Macphail continued to represent rural Grey county, Ontario, in the federal House of Commons until the election of March 1940. She then went on to represent the Toronto-area riding of York East in the Ontario provincial legislature, 1943–45, 1948–51. She died in a Toronto duplex in 1954, after struggling to support herself during her last few years "by journalism, public speaking and organizing for the Ontario CCF." She was an ardent and outspoken advocate for all manner of progressive causes and, as Naomi Black has put it, "though modern accounts have tended to deny it, in her own time ... recognized as a feminist." In this photograph she is sharing a rare wartime political platform with Mitch Hepburn, who was, by June 1941, already in his lamentable dotage as the Liberal populist premier of Ontario and (as the press liked to say) "Canada's Huey Long."

CTA, G&M, SC 266-74527

RICE BOWL FESTIVAL, JULY 11, 1941. Even in the capital city of Ontario it was the Second *World* War. These "pretty Chinese maidens, daughters of prominent citizens" of Toronto's "Chinese community" (the earlier "colony" has by now faded from the press) adorned a gathering at Convocation Hall on the university campus, held to raise funds for "China's cause in its battle against the Japanese invaders." The repeal of Canada's repressive Chinese Immigration Act of 1923 was still some half a dozen years off. But some young Toronto women of Chinese descent actually had managed to grow up in the city since the First World War. According to the report of the day in the *Globe*, the particular examples here are (left to right): Lai-Yen Mark, Phyllis Chu, Dores Joe, Mae Lee, Mildred Quan, and Jessie Lee.

CTA, G&M, SC 266-74892

"BLOSSOM TIME" AT THE ROYAL ALEX, MAY 9, 1941. The names in this case are (left to right): Nancy Leith (Bowmore Road), Gwendolyn Dainty (Lonsdale Road), Doris Hartman (Kingston Road), Irene Flint (Kennedy Park Road), and Sally Rhynas (Glenview Avenue). They are the semi-finalists in local auditions "for inclusion in the personnel of the 'Blossom Time' company," scheduled to start performing "a week from coming Monday" at the Royal Alexandra theatre on King Street. When it was built in the early twentieth century, the Royal Alex was the first air-conditioned and completely fireproof theatre in the world. In the late twentieth century, it would go on to become the first altogether elegant piece in the Toronto-based empire of the Mirvish family, whose crowning achievement has been the purchase of the Old Vic in London. Among the star-struck young Toronto women in this particular photograph from May 1941, only Sally Rhynas (far right) and perhaps the girl next to her (Irene Flint — the subsequent press reports are confusing) were actually included in the personnel of the "Blossom Time" company in the end.

CTA, G&M, SC 266-73565*

TORONTO GIRLS TO COOKSVILLE FARM, JULY 13, 1943. These are, according to the report in the *Globe*, "three of the girls who will spend thirteen weeks on 'help-the-farmer' holidays," during the summer that Benito Mussolini fell from power in Italy. Olivia Lubbock (left) lived on Avondale Road, near Yonge and Bloor; Joan Jackson's home was on Roxborough Street, not too far north of Olivia; and Ruth Smith lived on Yonge Street much further north, in North York township, beyond Sheppard Avenue. Filling in for young men who were off at war, they spent the summer of 1943 working on farms in the Cooksville area, a bit west of Toronto. Like all such "farmerettes," they wore a "khaki uniform, consisting of slacks or shorts and blouses."

CTA, G&M, SC 266-86283

JUNE CALLWOOD AND TRENT FRAYNE, MAY 2, 1944. The happy couple would be married just eleven days after this photograph was taken, on May 13. They would both go on to become prominent journalists in postwar Toronto, with careers that lasted well into the late twentieth century. June Callwood, who was born in Chatham, Ontario, became particularly known for her articles in *Maclean's* magazine during the 1950s, and then began to combine her journalism with social activism in the 1960s. She went on to write a number of books, including *The Law Is Not for Women* (1976), *Portrait of Canada* (1981), and *Twelve Weeks in Spring* (1986).

CTA, G&M, SC 266-90413

"VE DAY" ON BAY STREET, MAY 7, 1945. General Jodl made the final capitulation of Germany to Dwight Eisenhower on May 7, near Reims in France, and that is what these downtown Toronto working women and others are celebrating. In the textbooks, however, the "War in Europe" did not finally "end" until the next day, May 8, when Wilhelm Von Keitel surrendered to General Zhukov of the USSR, near the city of Berlin. According to the war historians Douglas and Greenhous, by the end of the Second World War, Canada was at least a little more than "the rather insignificant state the world had known in 1939 ... It had come out of the shadows." The women in Canada's second-largest city of Toronto had begun to come out of some shadows, too.

CTA, G&M, SC 266-96241

"I'M NOT MARRIED," AUGUST 14, 1945 (above). The war in Europe had ended on May 7 (or, more exactly, May 8). But the end of the World War only came with the surrender of Japan on August 14. And this is what the Toronto group here is celebrating. The caption to the photograph, in the *Globe* the next day, tells the story: "In case you need another hint, boys, the girls are looking for handsome escorts with whom to celebrate V Day. Left to right are AB. George House — looking definitely interested — June Purvis, June Fry, and Pte. Murray Small, all of Toronto. They were among the thousands of Torontonians who celebrated happily but in orderly fashion yesterday."

CTA, G&M, SC 266-98424

AT QUEEN'S PARK, SEPTEMBER 14, 1945 (opposite). These four Toronto women — (left to right) Thelma Nash, Gladys Gibson, Jean Noble, and "Barney" Hall — were "some of the girl workers who paraded with placards" during an address by the still comparatively new Progressive Conservative premier of Ontario, George Drew, in front of the provincial legislature. The premier "promised every assistance within the power of the Provincial Government." A September 1945 survey by the Canadian Institute of Public Opinion, however, reported that, at this point in the twentieth century, only 20 percent of Canadians supported full "equal opportunities" for men and women in the workplace, while 60 percent "said men should have preference." Women would, nonetheless, gradually come to play increasingly prominent roles in the Toronto labour force, during the generation that followed the Second World War.

CTA, G&M, SC 266-98982

MAKE
WARTIME
FACTORIES
GIVE
PEACETIME
JOBS
UNITED
STEELWORKERS
OF
AMERICA

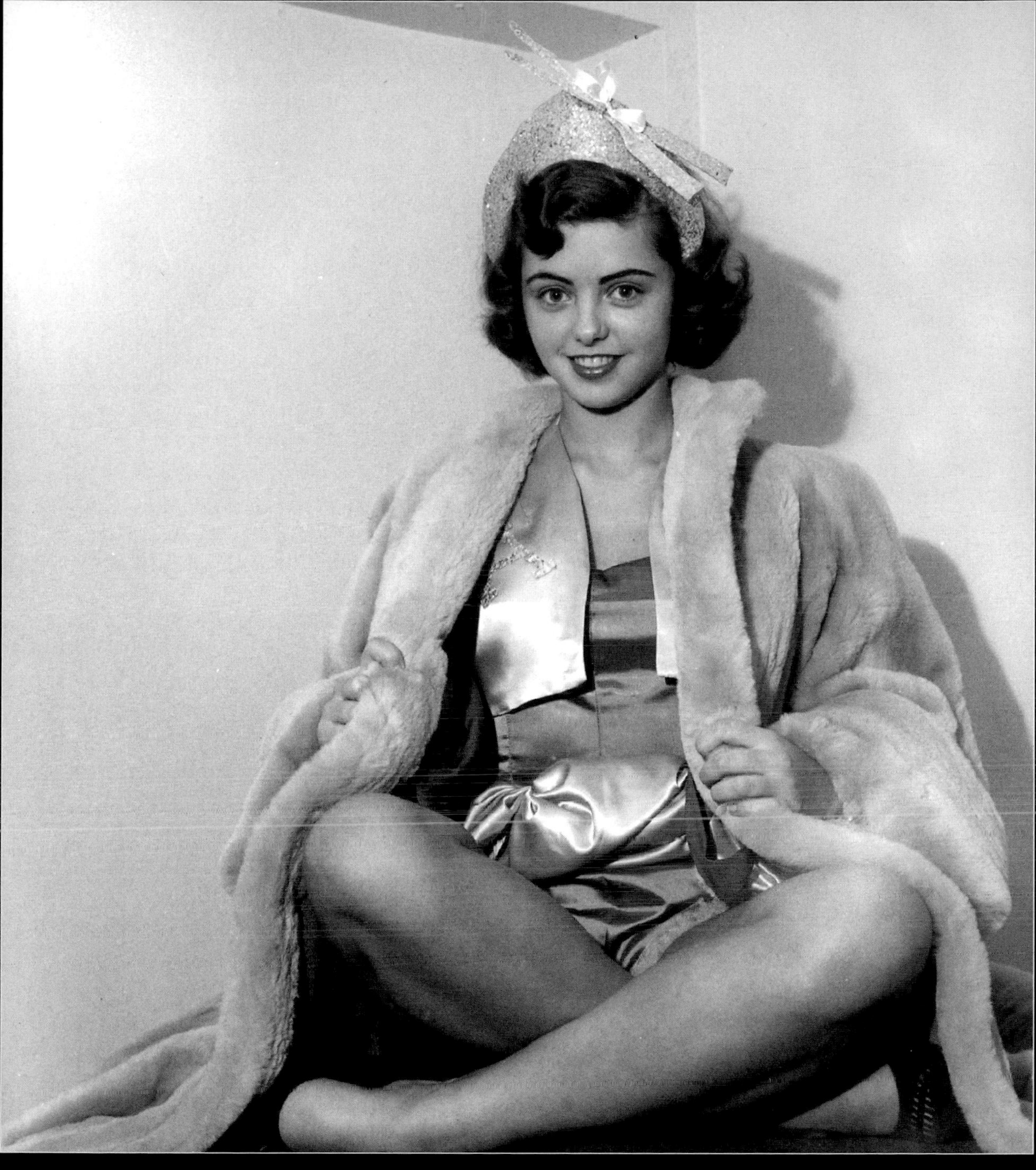

JEANETTE LASTOWSKA, CENTRAL HIGH SCHOOL OF COMMERCE STUDENT, MISS TORONTO ARGONAUT 1951, AND TORONTO'S ENTRY IN FIRST CANADA-WIDE MISS GREY CUP CONTEST, NOVEMBER 23, 1951.

CTA, G&M, SC 266-145428

6 At the Edge of Change

Like the earlier global conflict of 1914–1918, the Second World War opened a lot of closed doors. And on the northwest shore of Lake Ontario this time, the open doors would point in bold new directions. Between the late 1940s and the mid-1960s, the great sea change that leads to Toronto today began to stir.

The change developed on many different levels. Two quiet steps taken by the Canadian federal government in 1947 are cases in point. The first was the passage of legislation characterized in official sources as "the Canadian Citizenship Act ... the first independent naturalization law to be enacted in the Commonwealth ... which created the status of a Canadian citizen as distinct from that of a British subject." The second was the rescinding of the repressive Chinese Immigration Act of 1923 — a very early sign of new directions that ultimately led to the increasingly diverse new waves of migration, which would do so much to shape the Toronto of the late twentieth century.

The sudden rise of the USA to dramatic global influence and the final decline of the old "British Empire and Commonwealth" both had big impacts on the city. Then there was the shift from the jazz age to the new age of rock and roll in the wider culture, somewhere in the late 1950s and early 1960s. The establishment of the new Municipality of Metropolitan Toronto in the summer of 1953 and the opening of the first leg of the Yonge subway in 1954, from Eglinton Avenue to Union Station, were big local events. Above all else, perhaps (and with only a few intermittent stumbles), virtually the entire generation from 1945 to 1975 played host to a great new economic boom — deeper, more innovative, and more sustained than virtually all its Toronto ancestors.

The deepest truth about bold new directions, however, takes time to become clear. In the late 1940s and 1950s, and even the early 1960s, the gathering sea change in the city proper and its growing suburbs was still just an underground trend. Suddenly there were television aerials, big airplanes, and more than a hundred thousand new Torontonians from Italy. Yet when you look at their pictures, the lives of Toronto women seem to have remained much as they were at the start of the Second World War. And in some subtle, inadvertent way this is what Miss Toronto Argonaut 1951 seems to be trying to tell us today: her city was at the edge of a new era that had not quite yet arrived.

WOMAN WAVING NYLON STOCKINGS, FEBRUARY 19, 1946. Wartime rationing in Toronto had not been too severe during the first half of the 1940s, but it had effectively abolished nylon stockings for women in the city. Deep in the winter of 1946, Kay Sandford is enthused about "the first postwar nylons which go on sale today." Whatever else, the long economically buoyant era of 1945–1975 that is just beginning here would be a great age of consumer goods, in virtually all of North America (in the old Toronto sense of "Canada and the United States"). When the first nylons went on sale in the city in February 1946, stores like Eaton's and Simpson's had "an elaborate set-up to handle crowds." And they were "counting on the Toronto crowds to behave because nylons are only stockings. But what stockings!"

CTA, G&M, SC 266-102216

ROLLER-SKATING, MUTUAL ARENA, LATE 1940s. The three postwar Toronto women in this case are (left to right): Betty Jane Pike, Lena Reaves, and Janet Howitt. Until the opening of Maple Leaf Gardens for the 1930–31 season, the old arena on Mutual Street, five blocks east of Yonge, downtown, had hosted National Hockey League games in Toronto. By the later 1940s it had become a roller rink, which attracted younger people from all over the old city proper, and even the less-remote suburbs. Mutual Arena as it appears here would also have a subsequent renovated career under the new name of The Terrace — which eventually offered facilities for roller-skating, ice-skating, and curling as well. Nowadays, the building has vanished altogether, and been replaced by a downtown housing development. To help keep warm memories of the old arena alive, space has been left in the development for a new roller rink. Alas, the space was still vacant when our photograph collection went to press.

CTA, G&M, SC 266-104327

DOREEN MESSIAS, SUNNYSIDE EASTER PARADE, EARLY 1950s (above). "Sunnyside Beach" was the fabled "poor man's Riviera" on Toronto's west-end waterfront, developed on filled land by the Toronto Harbour Commission and first opened at the start of the summer of 1922. In its heyday, it boasted "Band Concerts ... Amusement Devices and Games, Supervised Bathing Facilities, Canoeing and Boating, Terraced Tea Gardens and Dancing, Lakefront Promenade and Boulevard Drive." Much of this remained intact during the ten years that immediately followed the Second World War. As Ms. Messias demonstrates here, in the early 1950s the lakefront promenade at Sunnyside was still the setting for an annual Easter parade. In 1955, however, work began on the Queensway and on what would eventually be called the Gardiner Expressway. And almost all of the poor man's Riviera was dismantled, to accommodate the new multi-lane highway era of the automobile age.

CTA, G&M, SC 266-139162

MAE GENNO, DANFORTH TECHNICAL SCHOOL STUDENT AND MISS BY-LINE 1951, SPRING 1951 (opposite). In the 1950s, Miss By-line was chosen at an annual ball held jointly by the Toronto Men's Press Club and the Toronto branch of the Canadian Women's Press Club. The 1951 ball was attended by over three thousand people and "resembled a mixture of the Calgary Stampede and the Midway at the CNE." Mae Genno was eighteen years old at the time, and lived with her mother, father, and younger sister at 26 Fernwood Park Avenue in the east-end Beaches neighbourhood. She designed and made the dress she is wearing here.

CTA, G&M, SC 266-143141

MS. MICHELE LANDSBERG IN THE EARLY 1950s. Some forty years after this photograph was taken, Michele Landsberg's *Toronto Star* newspaper column on "urban life, contemporary feminism, politics and education" would be entertaining and educating many Toronto women (and men), and irritating others, with a unique panache. But in her first public career, she had started acting on CBC radio when she was nine years old. Here, a few years later, she is appearing in *Aladdin and the Princess* at the Hart House Theatre, produced and directed by the influential drama teacher Josephine Barrington. A few years later again, an untimely case of German measles thwarted Ms. Landsberg's television debut in the first TV drama produced by the CBC, and this ended her experiment with acting. Having already begun her more general education in "Toronto public schools and Toronto public library," she went on to study English Language and Literature at the University of Toronto. When she joined the staff of the *Globe and Mail* after graduating from U of T in 1962, her second and more enduring career in journalism began.

CTA, G&M, SC 266-142048

AT THE HELICONIAN CLUB IN YORKVILLE, 1950s. Mrs. R.S. Van Valkenberg, past president, is pouring tea for Pegi Brown and Beth Lockersby. The Toronto Heliconian Club had been founded "in 1909 to give women in the arts and letters an opportunity to meet socially and intellectually." The name was suggested by Toronto's resident English intellectual of the late nineteenth and early twentieth centuries, Goldwin Smith. It alludes to Mount Helicon in ancient Boeotia, "sacred to Apollo and the Muses who had a temple there" in classical Greek mythology.

CTA, G&M, SC 266-139029

MS. EILEEN O'SULLIVAN AT CHERRY BEACH, 1950s. *Silent Spring* by the US biologist Rachel Carson — "the world-famous bestseller about our ravaged environment and the man-made pollution that is imperiling all life on earth" — would not be published until 1962. And protecting the environment did not become a great popular cause until the later 1960s and earlier 1970s. But even in the 1950s, you didn't have to be a rocket scientist to know there was a problem. By this point, city officials had pronounced that seven of Toronto's eleven beaches were unsafe for swimming "because of excessive pollution." Along with such Toronto women as Eileen O'Sullivan, some politicians had already begun to get the message. A city alderman complained that the "miles of natural beach which Toronto originally possessed now have been lost due to dumping raw sewage into the lake." Soon enough, there would be help from Queen's Park as well. The Ontario Progressive Conservative premier of the day, Leslie Frost, had met US president, Dwight Eisenhower, at a dinner in Ottawa. Eisenhower told him: "You people have a great country here with great possibilities, so don't let them ruin your water." Frost thought about this a bit, and then established the Ontario Water Resources Commission in 1956.

CTA, G&M, SC 266-143896

MARILYN BELL SURROUNDED BY GIFTS, 1954. Polluted or otherwise, Lake Ontario was still a place where one particular young Toronto woman of the 1950s did a lot of swimming. In the summer of 1954, the CNE and the *Telegram* offered the noted California marathon swimmer, Florence Chadwick, ten thousand dollars to swim across the lake. Then Winnie Roach Leuszler, of St. Thomas, Ontario, and the sixteen-year-old Marilyn Bell, of Toronto, challenged Ms. Chadwick. At first, the *Telegram* refused to recognize the challenge, but the *Daily Star* soon announced that it would underwrite the challengers' expenses. Late on the evening of September 8, the three swimmers left Youngstown, NY, on "the American side." Almost immediately, they had to battle twelve-foot waves. Chadwick and Leuszler gave up within hours, but the freckle-faced Marilyn Bell struggled on. She swam through the night and all the next day, battling high waves and numbing cold. Regular progress reports on the radio quickly spread the news of her odyssey throughout the city she was swimming towards. A crowd of over one hundred thousand had gathered to greet her when she finally touched the CNE breakwater at 8:06 PM, September 9. She had covered the thirty-two miles from Youngstown to Toronto in some twenty-one hours, and become the first person to swim across the fourth largest of the North American Great Lakes. To mark the achievement, she was showered with close to fifty thousand dollars worth of prizes and gifts.

CNE Archives, Biography Files

WOMEN'S FASHIONS AT THE DON JAIL, 1950s. Mid-twentieth-century Toronto was determined to do everything right, and this apparently included making sure that Toronto women prisoners at the since-retired Don Jail (just east of the Don River on Gerrard Street) had proper clothes to wear. This prescribed uniform was made by the inmates. The model here, however (Miss Joanne Dougall), is not an inmate herself, and was just visiting her uncle, Jail Governor Charles Sanderson.

CTA, G&M, SC 266-142276

BARBARA ELIZABETH MERCER: PORTRAIT OF THE ARTIST AS A YOUNG WOMAN, LATE 1950s. The painter Barbara Elizabeth Mercer, born in Galt, Ontario, in 1933, had her first solo exhibition at The House of Prints and the Centre Stage Theatre in Toronto in 1962. Her subsequent career took her to New York and San Francisco for a time, and then back to Toronto, where she worked with the Canadian Opera Company, the CBC, the National Ballet of Canada, the St. Lawrence Centre for the Arts, and TV Ontario. By the late 1970s, she was painting full time. In the 1980s her work was strongly influence by her experience among the glacial moraines of the Caledon hills, just north-west of Metropolitan Toronto, at a retreat she called Spirit Pond. Today she lives and works in Old Cabbagetown.

Barbara Elizabeth Mercer, Private Collection

ITALIAN BANQUET HALL, 1960s. In the saga of the new great migrations to Toronto that followed the Second World War, the Italians were the largest of various groups from Europe — Czech, German, Greek, Hungarian, Macedonian, Polish, Portuguese, Ukrainian, and on and on. Italians were the largest by a considerable margin, however, and it was in the 1950s that Toronto really started to become a centre for one of the world's largest populations of Italian descent, outside Italy, itself. By 1961 some 11.6 percent of all the people living in the old city proper were reporting Italian origins, up from 2.7 percent in 1951. Even in the wider, new Municipality of Metropolitan Toronto, the relative weight of the Italian-origin population more than tripled between 1951 and 1961. "One of the best things" that happened to the city, the inter-war nostalgist Robert Thomas Allen wrote in the early 1960s, was the influx of people from "Europe, who have helped Toronto grow up and have lightened the tone of the dour middle-class Scotch-English-Irish Canadian core that gave off a dull thud when I was a boy."

MHSO/PC

THE BRAITHWAITE FAMILY ON THEIR WAY HOME FROM CHURCH, 1963. By the middle of the 1960s, some new migrants from various parts of the Caribbean, Africa, and South and East Asia had also begun to arrive in the city. And, as in so many other parts of twentieth-century Toronto at the edge of change, there were some older traditions to greet the new trends. In the Braithwaite family of Scarborough here, mother Rella is from an old Ontario family. Father Bob was born in Montreal, and came to Ontario when he was stationed at Camp Borden during the Second World War. In the 1970s, Rella Braithwaite would write a column on black history for the Toronto publication *Contrast.* She is the author of *The Black Woman in Canada* (1976) and, with co-author, Tess Benn Ireland, *Some Black Women* (1993). The children in this 1963 photograph are: Brian (in the back at the left), Victor (between his mother and father), Cecil (at the front), Diana (immediately in front of her mother), and Charlane (at front, holding hands with Cecil). The picture was taken by the family's eldest daughter, Valerie.

Rella Braithwaite, Private Collection

BATH
SHEETS
6.77

7 The New Metropolis

By the late 1960s, it had become clear enough that the great postwar boom was transforming Toronto altogether. The population of the old city proper had remained comparatively stable since the early 1930s, at somewhere around 650,000 people. But the old "Toronto and its suburbs," as reorganized into the new municipal federation of Metropolitan Toronto in 1953, grew from some 1.1 million in 1951 to 1.6 million in 1961 to 2.1 million in 1971.

By the early 1970s, the main thrust of growth in the wider Toronto region had already spilled over into the exurbs beyond the new metropolitan municipality. Toronto in its widest sense was known to federal government statisticians as the Toronto Census Metropolitan Area, and eventually to Ontario provincial government officials as the (somewhat more expansive) Greater Toronto Area (or "GTA"). The population of Metro Toronto would continue to hover around 2.1 or 2.2 million. But by the early 1980s, there were more than 3.4 million people living in the late twentieth-century GTA.

By the middle of the 1970s, Toronto had at last surpassed Montreal as Canada's most-populous metropolitan region. It now qualified as one of the top ten markets in all of North America as well. And increasingly "global" migrations had also really begun to transform the "*British* American" city of the nineteenth and earlier twentieth centuries into a pot-pourri of cultural diversity. In the 1981 census, a mere 46.0% of the residents of Metropolitan Toronto reported so-called British ethnic origins, followed by 11.7% reporting Italian origins, 4.9% Jewish, 3.9% Chinese, 3.5% Portuguese, 3.0% Greek, 2.9% African, 2.6% German, another 2.6% Indo-Pakistani, 2.5% French, 1.9% Polish, another 1.9% Ukrainian, 1.8% Balkan, 1.1% Spanish and Latin American, another 1.1% Philippino, and on *ad infinitum.*

In the midst of all this ferment, female participation in the Metropolitan Toronto labour force rose to dramatic new heights. In 1951 just over a third of working-age women had jobs. By 1981 the proportion was just under 60 percent. The majority were now in the workplace. There were local representatives of the second sex in business, politics, the media, and in culture and the arts. The domestic scientists of an earlier era were bringing their various talents into wider worlds. More and more of the Toronto women who had merely become more daring in the 1920s grasped the mantle of "liberation," at last.

OPENING OF SKATING RINK, NEW CITY HALL, NOVEMBER 29, 1964. If you had to choose a single point at which the new metropolis finally arrived, the opening of the new city hall in 1965 (also the year that Canada at last got its very own flag) is probably good enough. Construction had begun in 1961, after an international competition that examined 532 different plans and then settled on the unique design by Viljo Revell of Finland. When the skating rink on Nathan Phillips Square in front was opened for business, in the late fall of 1964, construction on the actual buildings was still in progress (which explains the crane at the top of this photograph).

CTA, Toronto Fire Department Fonds, RG 10-78521

FASHION FILE AT THE CNE, MID-TO-LATE 1960s. The surviving evidence is that, at some point in the last half of the 1960s, some eighty young Toronto women vied for a chance to model at the CNE fashion show in the Queen Elizabeth Theatre. And the winners were (clockwise from six o'clock): Ulla Moreland, Jean MacDonald, Jean Williams, Sharon Marshal, Mary Trudeau, Maggie Flynn, Christie Matt, Jane Riddell, Joyce Young, and Ene Riisna.

CNE Archives, Canada Pictures Ltd., RG 4-0-3-0-79

NORA VAUGHAN IN HER SIXTIES, IN THE 1960s. Nora Vaughan was "a character who escaped from a Scott Fitzgerald novel and somehow landed in Rosedale," as the journalist Robert Fulford once put it. After receiving the University of Toronto's first master's degree in Chinese archaeology, she had become the first woman buyer for Eaton's department stores in the 1920s. She quit her job when she married O.D. Vaughan, a key figure in Eaton's senior management from the 1930s to his retirement in 1961, and then cultivated her broad interests in art, culture, philanthropy, and world travel. By the 1960s, the new metropolis in Toronto was more or less starting to appreciate her kind of talent. Nora and O.D. Vaughan's house on Beaumont Road could handle 140 guests, and became a favourite setting for the adventures recounted by the later twentieth-century *Globe and Mail* society columnist, Zena Cherry. Robert Fulford has also noted that the house was Nora Vaughan's "small personal museum," with "sculpture by Brancusi, Giacometti and Hepworth, drawings by Picasso, Matisse, and Bracque, paintings by Milne, Coughtry, Town and many other Canadians," and "Chinese scrolls and Egyptian heads." Nora Vaughan had been born at the start of the century, in 1900, and she would live on until a few weeks before Christmas 1993. She left some $2 million worth of bequests, to the Ontario College of Art, the University of Toronto, the Royal Ontario Museum, and the Canadian National Institute for the Blind.

Bryan Vaughan, CM, Private Collection

DORIS ANDERSON AND THE STAFF AT *CHATELAINE,* 1972. The Toronto-based *Chatelaine* had begun its career as a Canadian women's magazine in 1928 with emphasis on the role of woman as homemaker. Like many similar magazines in both Canada and the United States, by the 1960s it had found that the old formula was no longer working. Doris Anderson had become editor in 1957, and the magazine survived as "the sole remaining women's magazine in Canada" by (as Ms. Anderson herself would relate) "responding more rapidly than its US competitors to the concerns of women joining the work force and the beginning of the women's movement." In the group at the left of this photograph are: Doris Anderson, Jean Wright, Keith Branscombe, and Evelyn Stoynoff. In the group at the right are (by row, left to right): front row — Paula Weber, Versey Chapman, Sherrill Becker; second row — Barbara West, Donna Matthews; third row — Elaine Collett, Una Abrahamson, Wanda Nelles, Eveleen Dollery; back row — Breda Harding, Annabelle King, Robin Reid, Carol Buffett. The artwork in the background on the left is a blow-up of a Harold Town print.

Courtesy of *Chatelaine* © Maclean Hunter Publishing Ltd.

BETTY KENNEDY AND FRIEND, CFRB, EARLY 1970s (above). Betty Kennedy was born and raised in Canada's national capital at Ottawa, but she joined the staff at CFRB radio in Toronto in 1959. From then until her retirement in 1986, she produced and hosted a daily hour-long public affairs program, which had prime ministers and many other newsworthy figures as guests. In 1961 she had also joined the panel on what would become Canada's longest-running TV program, "Front Page Challenge," and she would remain with this show until its retirement in 1995. Somewhere along the way, she found time to serve on an impressive assortment of public and private boards and commissions, write two books, and raise four children as well. Today she lives in Milton, in the exurban outer reaches of the Greater Toronto Area.

Betty Kennedy, Private Collection

SUHANA MEHARCHAND AND FRIEND, FAIRVIEW MALL, 1970 (opposite). While Betty Kennedy was at work in the new metropolis, one of her successors in the city's broadcast media had other things on her mind. Suhana Meharchand's family had come to Toronto from Durban, South Africa, in the late 1960s. (It was snowing when they arrived, and her mother was dressed just in a sari.) Suhana was eight years old when this photograph was taken at Fairview Mall in North York. She would later study broadcast journalism at Ryerson Polytechnical Institute, and start working for CBC-TV in 1987. After stints with stations in Ottawa, Hamilton, and Windsor, she was appointed anchor of the "CBC Evening News" in Toronto in 1995 (just after Betty Kennedy finished her last season with "Front Page Challenge"). Suhana today lives in North Toronto with her husband and two children. She was expecting a third child when our photograph collection went to press.

Suhana Meharchand, Private Collection

15446

ANNEMARIE SMITH ON HER BROTHER'S MOTORCYCLE, 1971. When this photograph was taken, Annemarie Smith was a nurse at Princess Margaret Hospital, and lived in "the hippy area" near Jarvis and Gloucester in downtown Toronto. The picture itself, however, was shot at her grandparents' fiftieth anniversary party in Grand Bend, Ontario. Her mother was telling her not to ride on her brother's motorcycle and, liberated Toronto woman of the 1970s that Annemarie was, she was declining to take the advice. She would later leave nursing for pharmaceutical sales, and then later again became a full-time mother of two sons. She now lives in Scarborough and, as an avocation, works part-time as a dog trainer for the St. John's Ambulance "therapy dog" program for handicapped children.

Alex MacDonald, Photographer (AMP)

WINSOME MCFARLANE AND THOR, ROCHDALE COLLEGE, 1972. Winsome McFarlane is the daughter of a Jamaican family that had migrated to Montreal. Following her parents' advice about economic security, she trained and then worked as a nurse in Montreal before she came to Toronto in 1971. In the new metropolis, she was at first more attracted to the innovative "vibrations" at Rochdale College — the University of Toronto's bid to respond creatively to the flower-power of the later 1960s. Winsome worked in the rental office at Rochdale, and found that if she took Thor along when she went to collect rents "people were more willing to pay." She was fascinated by the great variety of people at Rochdale and their search for new ways, but in the end it didn't work. In the mid-1970s, she embarked on a varied career of her own — modelling, acting on TV, selling real estate, running a pet store, and operating a horse farm in Unionville. She finally remembered her parents' advice and returned to nursing. Her current address is just east of the most easterly old-city limits, where she lives with her teenage daughter.

AMP

RAYNETTE COKER, MISS TORONTO UNITED APPEAL 1973. As it happens, the new metropolis's Miss United Appeal 1973 lived in exactly the same east-end Beaches house that Miss By-line had lived in back in the early 1950s (see page 94). Raynette Coker comes from a family that has been in Toronto "ever since the time when there were only about a hundred black families in the city." Raynette was a social worker at Dixon Hall in the near east end of the old city in 1973. Nowadays she runs an open-custody facility for young offenders. She is still living in the same Beaches house, with her almost teenage son.

Raynette Coker, Private Collection

SUKI ULMAN, GIVING PEACE A CHANCE ON INDIAN ROAD, 1975. Candles were actually lit on some Toronto streets the night John Lennon died in New York City. And the sign behind Suki Ulman here had been made for an earlier John and Yoko concert at Varsity Stadium. The photograph was taken on the almost mystical Indian Road, near High Park in the west end. Suki herself has gone on to become a writer and photographer, with a particular interest in travel to faraway parts of the global village. She has visited, photographed, and written about such places as Borneo, India, Indonesia, Malaysia, and Tibet in connection with her work. When she isn't travelling today, she lives in the St. Clair-Oakwood neighbourhood, just inside the old city of York.

AMP

TWIN SISTERS, 1976. The father of the twin sisters, Anne (left) and Marta Howard, was headmaster of the prep school at the all-male Upper Canada College from the mid-1960s to the mid-1980s. And they both attended the all-female Bishop Strachan School (somewhat to the west on the same street, in what is now midtown Toronto in the old city). They were visiting friends still further west, on Wychwood Avenue, when this picture was taken in 1976. Anne had just finished the Radio and Television Arts course at Ryerson, and Marta was working for the McClelland and Stewart publishing house. Later on, in the 1980s, Anne was a producer and founding member of "The New Music" — precursor of the present-day "MuchMusic" cable channel operated by CITY-TV. Marta now lives in St. Albert, Alberta, and has two children. Anne remains a Toronto woman, living in the Davisville and Yonge area, and has plans to make a film.

AMP

MEDITERRANEAN TORONTO AT COLLEGE AND CLINTON STREETS, 1980. The names of all three ladies here are alas unknown, but the picture still suggests something about the later twentieth century fate of the neighbourhood where the CBC-TV comics Johnny Wayne and Frank Shuster had grown up, between the two world wars. In fact, though the climate is somewhat different, Toronto is at about the same global latitude as Monaco on the Mediterranean Sea. And by 1980, there were various parts of the new metropolis where the culture of Mediterranean Europe had, metaphorically or spiritually at least, begun to melt the ice and snow of the Canadian winter. By this point as well, Mediterranean Toronto had already begun to spread well beyond the historic reception areas for new migrants in the city proper, into various parts of the metropolitan municipality and the still wider GTA. But older people especially still remained in the older neighbourhoods.

David Levine Photograph, MHSO/PC

DONE

BREAKING THE GLASS CEILING AT THE CITY OF NORTH YORK, 1980 (above). By 1980, increasing numbers of Toronto women had begun to assume managerial positions in the public and private sectors of the mainstream local economy. Anna DiRuscio, director of information services for the then quite recently rechristened city of North York, was one of them. And she had an engaging concern to keep her hard-earned rise up the corporate ladder in some suitable perspective. As she explains today, "Keeping a sense of humour has always been part of my approach to corporate public relations culture. Work hard but have fun. Don't take life too seriously."

City of North York Archives

AT THE WOMEN'S PRESS, ca. 1979 (opposite). At the height of the Toronto radical political scene in 1972 (also the year that David Crombie became the "tiny perfect mayor" of the old city proper), a group of local feminist activists had formed a collective to publish a single anthology called *Women Unite.* The collective went on to become The Women's Press — a diverse assortment of "staff and volunteers," as founding member, Liz Martin, explains, "determined to articulate the concerns of the burgeoning feminist movement." And the Women's Press in Toronto also became "one of the first North American book publishers to actively promote non-sexist and non-racist writing for children." By 1988, when internal political upheaval led to the formation of a successor organization known as Second Story Press, the original collective had published some eighty different titles. The members of the group in this late 1970s photograph are (by row, from left to right): top row — Lois Pike, Meg Luxton, Wendy Donner, Judy Skinner; third row — Margie Wolfe, Naomi Wall, Peggy McDonough; second row — Jane Springer, Bonnie Fox, Brenda Roman; front — Liz Martin.

Liz Martin, Private Collection

FLOWERS ON THE DANFORTH IN THE 1990s (LEFT TO RIGHT): ALICIA MAUTI AND HER DAUGHTER, SOPHIA, FIONA BAPTISTE, MAUREEN CONCEPCION, TESSAMA ALLEYNE, ON DANFORTH AVENUE AT EAST LYNN.

AMP

8 On the Cusp

The changes unleashed on the Toronto of an earlier era by the 1896–1913 great boom and the First World War were, among other things, blunted and even stopped short by the Great Depression of the 1930s. But there has been no altogether analogous phenomenon to blunt and stop short the changes wrought by the Second World War and the great boom of 1945–1975.

The local scene was certainly affected by one kind of economic recession in the late 1970s and early 1980s. This was followed by an all-too-brief new boom in the later 1980s, and then another kind of recession in the earlier 1990s. Yet nothing, it seems, has or can stop the pace of change at the edge of the twenty-first century. And nowadays, Canada's most populous and still-growing metropolitan region must cope with such various dramatic new issues as globalization and the Information Age, the very future of Canada and Quebec itself, and last, but by no means least, the future of the 1998 Toronto megacity and the wider GTA, in its very own backyard.

Toronto today in its broadest sense also includes a great many more different human beings than it ever has before. In 1996 the old city proper (or the official pre-1998 city of Toronto) still had the approximately 650,000 people that it has had since the 1930s. And Metropolitan Toronto had just under 2.4 million people — or not too many more than it has had since the 1970s. But the more far-flung Greater Toronto Area was home to almost 4.7 million people — or close to a million more than a decade before. To take just one measure of the quite vast diversity of this current metropolitan humanity, in the 1991 federal census about 38% of all GTA residents were migrants from other countries. And, midway through 1997, some 61% of working-age women in the entire GTA, 62% in the pre-1998 city of Toronto, and a dramatic 68% in the exurban or so-called "905" zone of the GTA, beyond the old Metro Toronto, were in the labour force.

Like all other Torontonians, old and new, Toronto women have been digesting this increasingly dazzling change and variety as best they can. As the twentieth century comes to an end, they are on the cusp of some suitably mysterious new future. Exactly what this future will turn into is still not very clear. The only certainty is that Toronto women will continue to play a greater and greater part in whatever Toronto ultimately comes to be. And, nowadays, who would or could deny that this can only be an excellent thing?

KENSINGTON MARKET IN THE EARLY 1980s. Sixty years later, the 1920s "Jewish market on Kensington Ave. North of Dundas" (see page 54) was no longer as particularly Jewish as it used to be, but it was still a place where "vendors of wares of almost every imaginable sort" did business. The adjacent south Spadina strip was also not yet quite as immersed in Chinese culture as it would subsequently become (though the trend was in motion). Today there is talk about a new condominium development in the Kensington area itself, to accommodate young and restless downtown professionals. Once again, alas, the name of the early 1980s Toronto woman in the photograph is unknown.

David Levine Photograph, MHSO/PC

MARILYN LASTMAN, FIRST LADY OF THE CITY OF NORTH YORK, 1980s. If the established urbanity of the old city proper has had any rival in late twentieth-century Metropolitan Toronto, it has been the rising suburbanity of the new city of North York — with its new civic square and centre for the performing arts, just north of what used to be a rather dreary intersection at Yonge and Sheppard. Until the advent of the 1998 megacity, Marilyn Lastman's husband (whose family has roots in the Kensington market area) was mayor of North York for twenty-five consecutive years. She has an accompanying quarter-century record of public-spirited community and charity work in both the city of North York and Metro Toronto at large. The gown she is wearing here was made for the Helicon Ball charity gala. Ms. Lastman posed in it for the noted Canadian portrait photographer Arton Cavouk, whose family originally came to Canada from Egypt.

Arton Cavouk, Photographer, courtesy of Marilyn Lastman

MADAM JUSTICE ROSALIE ABELLA, DECEMBER 1989 (above). Born in Stuttgart, Germany, Rosalie Silberman Abella came to Canada with her family in 1950, when she was four years old. She graduated from the University of Toronto Law School in 1970, and was admitted to the Bar in Ontario in 1972. In 1976 she was appointed a judge of the Ontario Provincial Court (Family Division). And she became a justice of the Court of Appeal for Ontario in 1992. In 1983–84 she served as the sole commissioner for the Royal Commission on Equality in Employment and created the term and concept of "employment equity," which has subsequently figured in the practical public life of Canada, Northern Ireland, and New Zealand. She moderated the televised Leaders' Debate in the crucial 1988 Canadian federal election campaign. In 1992 she was Chief Rapporteur at the Halifax Constitutional Conference and Co-Chair at the Vancouver Concluding Constitutional Conference. In 1996 she became the first woman to receive the Distinguished Alumnus Award from the Faculty of Law at the University of Toronto. Madam Justice Abella plays the piano for relaxation. She and her husband, Professor Irving Abella, of York University in Toronto, have two sons.

Rosalie Abella, Private Collection

THE NEW WOMAN IN POLITICS, OLIVIA CHOW IN THE SUMMER OF 1987 (opposite). Municipal politics in Toronto became more attractive when Olivia Chow was first elected as a public school trustee in 1985. She went on to become Metro councillor for the "Downtown Ward" in 1991. In the 1970s, she had worked as a waitress and taken a university degree in fine arts. Among many other things, she ran community programs at Woodgreen Centre in the 1980s, served as special assistant to the federal member of parliament, Dan Heap, and developed the vast contacts that would make her such an effective local politician in the 1990s. Ms. Chow speaks fluent Cantonese as well as English. And, reminiscent of Margaret Clyne (wife of Jean Baptiste Rousseau in late eighteenth-century Toronto), she enjoys "extensive experience in white-water canoeing." She also enjoys karate, and is "slightly obsessed with gardening and reading."

AMP

MISS ITALIA IN THE WORLD CANADA, 1995, 1996, 1997. By the time of the 1991 census, the Chinese had succeeded the Italians as the largest group of recent migrants in the old city proper, and the great weight of Toronto's increasingly established Italian community had moved into the suburbs and the exurbs of the GTA. Among those reporting single origins, Italians remained the largest group after the so-called British, in both Metro Toronto and the GTA. But people reporting "multiple origins" were now larger than all other single groups. Winners of the Miss Italia Canada contest, held in Toronto, go on to compete in the Miss Italia in the World contest in Italy. Miss Italia Canada 1995, Adriana Mobile, was the first Italian-Canadian woman to qualify in the top ten for Miss Italia in the World. And both Miss Italia Canada 1996 (Maria Christina Bruno) and 1997 (Rossanna Tassone) were first runner-ups for Miss Italia in the World. All three Miss Italia Canada winners here have been or still are students at York University in Toronto as well.

Courtesy of Vince Papa, Mediawerx Creative Group Inc.

CARIBBEAN TORONTO MEETS MEDITERRANEAN TORONTO IN THE 1990s. Wendy Rodie (on the left with her two children) came to Toronto from Guyana as a young girl in the late 1960s. The parents of Karen Csida (centre) came from Greece (though her Hungarian last name comes from her husband). Beno Mussenden (right) came to Toronto from Guyana in the early 1990s. Wendy, who lives in Scarborough, is a nurse, and Beno is a student at G.L. Roberts in Oshawa, and a model in her spare time. Karen lives on the Danforth, but is establishing a fitness centre in Mississauga (where one of her sisters lives already), and thinks she will move there soon. On this particular occasion, the Toronto women and children in this photograph were all out shopping in the old-city east end.

AMP

ALEX MACDONALD'S WOMEN'S MOVEMENT, LYND AVENUE, 1991. Energy policy consultant and part-time photographer Alex MacDonald is a man who, like John Boyd in an earlier era, very much likes Toronto women. And in the early 1990s, he gave a party for some of his favourite representatives of the species, at his house in the Dundas Street West/Howard Park area. The guests included (back row, left to right): Sheila White, community resource coordinator for North York mayor, Mel Lastman; Marilyn Rivers, a single mother currently working on a master's degree; Jennifer Patterson, who has "gone from bartending in the 1970s and 1980s to investment banking in the 1990s;" Nikki Morison, who has worked in various research and sales positions at the CBC for twenty-two years; Edith Fraser, an "equalist and cultural worker," employed by the University of Toronto; and Cheryl Couling, caterer and supplier of baked goods to dessert cafés. In the front of the picture, just ahead of Alex, are Lindsay Mitchell (left), "a former horticulturalist and proponent of animal rights and social justice, who co-organized Project Indigenous Restoration 1991–92," and Pat Mohans, a fashion designer and artist, whose paintings focus on women's issues.

AMP

ISOBEL HOFFMANN: TORONTO WOMAN ENTREPRENEUR OF THE YEAR, 1997. Isobel Hoffmann grew up in Switzerland and Portugal, and came to Canada in her late teens in 1976. Because her English was still shaky, she chose to study mathematics at the University of Toronto, and the choice proved fortuitous. She finished her academic training with a master's degree in computer science and education. Then in 1985, she began Hoffmann and Associates, which has gone on to become one of Canada's largest developers of multimedia software products. Ms. Hoffmann's young son, Nikolai, was the inspiration behind the internationally acclaimed Nikolai's Adventure Series — her own initial adventure into children's recreational software. "Nikolai's Trains," the first title in the series, has sold some two hundred thousand copies worldwide. In 1997 Ms. Hoffmann received the Canadian Woman Entrepreneur of the Year Award from the Faculty of Management at the University of Toronto. As it happens, she is not the first woman in her family to open new ground. In another time and place, her grandmother became the first female orchestra conductor in Europe.

Isobel Hoffmann, Private Collection

MOTHER AND DAUGHTER ON THE BEACHES BOARDWALK, 1990s. Paris Quinn (right) was born in Dublin, Ireland, and her daughter, Siobhan, was born in Auckland, New Zealand. The family subsequently moved to Australia and then in 1987, when Siobhan was nine years old, from Australia to Toronto. After some two decades as a full-time mother, Paris has just started a job with the *Beaches Town Crier*. And Siobhan is just starting Radio and Television Arts at Ryerson, in downtown Toronto.

Paris Quinn, Private Collection

SOMALI SHASH SAR IN NORTH YORK, SUMMER 1997. Like so many other places from which people who now live in Toronto have come, the northwestern region of present-day Somalia used to be a part of the British empire. Zainab Abdi (bottom left), who came to Toronto from Somalia in the early 1990s, was married seven days before this photograph was taken. Following Somali tradition, Amina Guled (right) and other married women friends have assembled to instruct Ms. Abdi in the correct style for wearing the shash or head scarf in the traditional Somali dress for married women. Another Somali tradition (quite in keeping with the habits of increasing numbers of Toronto women at large today) is that married women retain their maiden surnames.

Rashid Farrah, Private Collection

AT MAHARANI FASHIONS ON GERRARD STREET, 1997. The fiftieth anniversary of the independence of India in 1997 was also the fiftieth anniversary of the first Canadian Citizenship Act, passed just after the Second World War in 1947 (see page 91). Most of the more than two hundred thousand people of South Asian (or "East Indian") descent who now live in the Greater Toronto Area reside outside the old city proper — especially in Mississauga, Scarborough, North York, Brampton, and Etobicoke. But the "Little India" commercial strip on Gerrard just west of Coxwell nonetheless attracts many shoppers from the wider GTA. The merchant ladies here are (left to right): Daisy Chowdhury (originally from Calcutta and now living in Scarborough), Anshu Batra (from Delhi and now in Brampton), Jaswant Narang (from the Punjab and now, as an exception to the wider rule, on Gerrard Street), and Selvi Sornakumar (from Sri Lanka and now in Scarborough).

AMP

THREE FRENCH CANADIANS IN THEIR SECOND HOME, LATER 1990s. Nowadays, it seems, no self-respecting Québécois of either gender would ever move to the "anti-ville" in Toronto. But more than fifty-two thousand residents of the Greater Toronto Area reported French origins in the 1991 census, and it seems safe to assume that a great many of them were French Canadians. Jocelyne Gosselin MacFarlane (left), Antonine Cormier (centre), and Marie Auffrey (right) are Acadians from New Brunswick. In an earlier era, they all went to high school together in the Moncton area. Marie came to Toronto first, in the early 1970s, and Jocelyne and "Nin" arrived later in the same decade. Today they all work as teachers for the Metropolitan Toronto Separate School Board. They all still "feel Acadian," still speak Canada's other official language, and still keep up close ties with New Brunswick, which they still see as their first and happiest home. But Toronto is where they and their own most immediate families live now. It has become their second home, and they are happy enough about that. The Toronto art in the background here is a painting by Michael James Seward.

Natalie MacFarlane, Photographer

PAMELA WALLIN AND HER FRIEND, KITTY, LATE 1990s. One notable feature of Toronto in the late twentieth century is the vast influence of assorted bright lights among the city's resident media mafia from western Canada. And probably the brightest has been Pamela Wallin, from Wadena, Saskatchewan. Ms. Wallin graduated from the University of Regina, and earned a Certificate d'Études Françaises from the College of Bandol, France. Back in Canada, she took a job as a social worker at Prince Albert Penitentiary. But soon enough she was working for the CBC in Ottawa. In 1981 she became co-host of "Canada AM" on CTV. Four years later, she was the first woman Ottawa bureau chief in Canadian television history. By the early 1990s, she was back with CBC on "Prime Time News." She now hosts and produces "Pamela Wallin Live" on CBC Newsworld — a setting for some of the most intelligent and informative television in North America. Ms. Wallin is a fan of Marilyn Monroe and both she and Kitty live in midtown Toronto today .

Anne Bayin, Photographer

HER WORSHIP BARBARA HALL, LAST MAYOR OF THE OLD CITY OF TORONTO, 1996. Barbara Hall will go down in local history as the last mayor of the old city of Toronto "proper," that is now being replaced by the new megacity which takes effect on January 1, 1998. At the end of an era in which Toronto at last became Canada's largest metropolis, it also seems somehow fitting that Mayor Hall has a BA from the University of Victoria on Canada's Pacific coast — and that she began her working career in the late 1960s with the Company of Young Canadians in rural Nova Scotia, on Canada's Atlantic coast. Her subsequent community activism in the old city of Toronto, in the 1970s, 1980s, and early 1990s, has helped keep the historic core of the new metropolis a place fit to live as well as work in. As mayor since 1994, Ms. Hall has believed in talking problems out. This is (dare one say?) a "Toronto woman's approach," and who can doubt that it has served the old city well enough. In one way or another, it still has a role to play in the future, that lies so mysteriously, and so intriguingly, ahead.

Tony Bock, Photographer, *Toronto Star*

ON THE WATERFRONT AT BALMY BEACH, SUMMER 1997. As a kind of official proof that the age of innocence at the start of the twentieth century really has now ended forever, the courts have recently decided that women in all parts of Canada's most populous province, just like men, have the right to appear topless in public. And this is just one of a great many senses in which there are more interesting Toronto women today than there have ever been before. The particular examples here are (left to right): Angela Gordyn, Sandie Sherbanowski, and Alicia Mauti, who still like to return to the water's edge, where all of Toronto still begins.

AMP

Epilogue
MEGACITY PMS

To start with very quickly, we ought to confess that all three authors of this book have been, in their own quiet ways, opponents of the dreaded "megacity" — the creation of a new single city of Toronto within the boundaries of the old Metropolitan Toronto federation. We all voted No in the municipally organized 1997 metro-wide plebiscite on the issue, just like the great majority of those who turned out to vote.

Yet, as events have finally unfolded, the present management of the province of Ontario has proved determined to go ahead with its amalgamation plans. As of January 1, 1998, the city of Toronto is now a single municipality of some 2.4 million people, covering the entire old territory of the former Metro federation.

Democratic politics is impossible unless each of us accepts that, in all such matters, sometimes we will win and sometimes we will lose. In Canada provincial governments have the legal authority to reorganize local governments more or less at will. In the way in which it has gone about deciding on and creating the new megacity, the government of Ontario may or may not have overstepped the bounds of the more informal democratic conventions that have come to be associated with local government in Toronto. But the proper place for making judgements on this issue *is* the next provincial election.

Meanwhile, we former megacity opponents can only accept the new city of Toronto, and do as best we can to ensure that it does not in fact become the dinosaur we have been predicting. The only question we can put to the photographs in this book is just what should be done to keep the Toronto woman's habitat active and vital, and altogether alive?

As strange as it may seem, we do feel that the photographs have been talking to us about this subject. And so have a lot of people (Toronto women and even a few men) who have helped us find our way through a maze of public and private photographic archives. The message that we at least have finally heard goes right back to *Fortune* magazine's recent pronouncement that "internationally, no other metropolitan area combines favorable working and living conditions as well as Toronto." By the end of the twentieth century, Toronto has become one of the "great cities for doing business." But it has also remained, in "short, a good place for raising a family."

Megacity advocates, as we see it, have been emphasizing the working- and doing-business side of this equation. Megacity opponents have been emphasizing the "living" and "raising a family" side. And it is this living-as-well-as-working side of Toronto's past, present, and future that is stressed again and again, in so many different ways, by the photographs of Toronto women which appear in this book.

There are sensible things to be said on both sides of the equation. The last quarter of the twentieth century in Toronto has had various economic ups and downs — after the long boom that followed the Second World War (and that many of us still can't quite forget). Megacity advocates are on solid ground when they argue that this experience has shown just how important it is, for everyone who lives here, to worry about the economy of Toronto in all its senses, and to work hard to facilitate its continuing dynamism and long-term development and growth.

Yet our sense is that megacity opponents have been trying to say two things. The first is that there is not really much at all to suggest how creating a single new city of Toronto out of the old Metropolitan Toronto federation actually will improve economic growth prospects in any part of the present Greater Toronto Area.

The second point is that there is more than a little to suggest how turning the Metro federation into a single new city of Toronto *is* going to make it more difficult to attend to the living-and-raising-a-family side of the local recipe for big-city success. (In this connection, if you like, there are a great many senses in which "small *is* beautiful.") The photographs in this book have also been telling those of us who put it together that this other side of Toronto's past is just as important a part of any successful future it may have as the crucial economic base. Even *Fortune* magazine's characterization of what really gives Toronto an edge in the wider global village today implies that each side of the equation depends on the other. "Workers have known it for a while. And employers have finally caught on: the best and most productive employees are those who have a life outside the office."

And so the megacity message of this photograph collection, as we see it, is that effectively managing *both sides* of the equation will be the greatest challenge that the new city of Toronto political process, officially kicked off at the start of January 1998, will face. In the end the megacity has been so dreaded in old Toronto itself, because so many old Torontonians have feared it would somehow work against the twenty-first-century future of what Toronto women have done so much to create in the twentieth century. All of us, megacity opponents and advocates alike, still need to find some way of ensuring that this does not, in fact, take place.

A metropolis, of course, is a vast and complicated human community. And in still other ways again, the fate of old Toronto by itself is not really the key issue. The deepest argument for the megacity is that it is supposed to be just the first step in a response to the plain fact that, ever since the 1970s, the real growth of Toronto has been taking place in the exurbs, outside the boundaries of the old Metropolitan Toronto federation.

Consolidating Metro into a single new city of Toronto, the advocates seem to have been claiming (in their more logical moments, at least), is a logical first step in coming to grips with the various practical problems of managing metropolitan growth in the whole Greater Toronto Area of some 4.7 million people — from Lake Ontario north to the town of Georgina on the shores of Lake Simcoe, and from the municipality of Clarington in the east to the town of Burlington in the west.

Here, too, the complicated process of putting this photograph collection together — and the many intriguing Toronto women (and men) we have met along the way — have also put a few thoughts into our heads.

The 1912 hikers along Eglinton Avenue West, near Bathurst, or Miss Jennie Brown tending her cattle in the Runnymede area of 1923 show what Robert Thomas

Allen had in mind when he wrote that "the city didn't sprawl into the country then; the country came right into the city."

But nowadays the city *does* sprawl into the country: Betty Kennedy lives in Milton; Anshu Batra lives in Brampton; and Karen Csida, who grew up in the old-city east end, has plans to move to Mississauga, where her sister Anna already lives, and where her other sister Angela plans to live as well. The Toronto municipality with the largest share of people reporting Italian origins today is not in the old city or even the old Metro Toronto, but in the new city of Vaughan, in the so-called outer or "905" region of the GTA. The GO train leaves Union Station on Front Street and lands in Oakville or Streetsville or Pickering or Rouge Hill. According to labour force statistics, the housewife who practises domestic science full time is now actually a less-common figure in the new exurbs than she is in the old downtown.

All this takes us back to the geographical meaning of the word Toronto, that we pondered briefly in introducing our photograph collection at the very start of the book. And it may at first seem strange to say that the further ahead any place goes into the future, the further it also goes back into its own past. But there are several senses in which this, nonetheless, seems true.

Back in the past before the town of York — in the long and diverse era from the rise of new Iroquois villages on the north shore of Lake Ontario after 1650, down to the multiracial fur-trade romance of Jean-Baptiste Rousseau and the Mississauga in the early 1790s — "Toronto" did not imply any exact dot on the map.

In the seventeenth, eighteenth, and earlier nineteenth centuries, in fact, Toronto does seem to have referred to all or various parts of a far-flung geographic space, which probably has more in common with today's Greater Toronto Area than with any of the official cities of Toronto that have existed since 1834. What we now call Lake Simcoe is called "Lac Toronto" on some early French maps. It sometimes seems, as well, that Toronto may have been used to refer to the long canoe portage from Lake Ontario to Lake Simcoe itself. (And perhaps the meaning "trees in water" even evokes the combination of such things one would, at that time, find everywhere along this route.)

In a similar sense there are historic usages which suggest a Toronto that looks a bit like a triangle, with the apex at Lake Simcoe and the base running some distance along the north shore of Lake Ontario — again, much as the GTA does today. The present-day city of Mississauga used to be known as Toronto township. For a short time after the War of 1812, the post office at what is now Port Hope was known as "Toronto on Smith's Creek." And in the earlier 1830s, Port Hope itself toyed with the idea of adopting the name Toronto, before it settled in the end on Port Hope.

Thus, the place that the Toronto women of the twentieth century have come to and lived in has been a Toronto that is growing. The Toronto that is growing today is in the whole of the Greater Toronto Area (which probably is the most real Toronto of the more ancient past as well). Women from the more far-flung parts of this wider region have been helping to shape Toronto throughout even the more recent period covered by the photographs in this book. And those exurban parts of the GTA today, outside even the newest city of Toronto, are also the heirs of what the Toronto women of the twentieth century have done so much to create.

Finally, the human process of putting this photograph collection together has also put a few brief thoughts into our heads about the reputed great human divide in the wider Greater Toronto Area today. On the one hand, there are those who live in the inner parts of the region and use the long-distance telephone code "416." And then there are those who live in the outer exurban parts, and use the code "905" (and are, in some cases, still not certain that they want to be a part of any "Toronto area").

The most immediate great challenge of whatever new governmental and political or other process may or may not ultimately be established to preside over the affairs of the GTA today will no doubt be to bridge this great divide, in some creative and constructive way. And what has really begun to unify the GTA in this sense is the increasingly vast network of human relationships, that regularly enough cross over all the tense and uptight lines of urban-suburban-exurban division.

More and more people from all backgrounds who live or work in "416" have family and friends who live or work in "905," and vice-versa. At least some people have begun to look around the entire area, for all the various forms of entertainment and instruction and public involvement that make up Toronto civic culture today. It is probably in this emerging vast network of human relationships, our Toronto women photograph collection seems to be telling us, that those who are looking for the human will to bridge the assorted political and other chasms between "the new city" and "the new suburbs" will eventually find what they need.

Hopefully, there will be no more megacities. The various forms of diversity and variety that are latent in the Greater Toronto Area today will deepen and develop, rather than be smothered under some single cloud of greater metropolitan monotony (not unlike the various diverse and rival urban neighbourhoods, which some have always seen as the greatest attraction of the oldest city). But when some other authors come to put together a book of photographs celebrating the contribution of Simone de Beauvoir's second sex to the life of Toronto in the twenty-first century, it will no doubt be a lot longer and a lot bigger and a lot more complicated than this one. And this is the newest future of Toronto women, still looming on the horizon ahead.

GERRY AND BOBBIE, TWO SISTERS IN THE GREATER TORONTO AREA TODAY, LATE SUMMER 1997. Geralyn (left) and Roberta Wraith's late mother was an Ojibway from the Pays Plat reserve on the north shore of Lake Superior — the granddaughter of the Pays Plat chief, Joe Fisher. In the late seventeenth century, the "Ojibway conquest" had pushed the Iroquois off the north shore of Lake Ontario. The Ojibway nation of the Mississauga was still the single-largest group of people in the Toronto region when the town of York was founded in 1793. Gerry and Bobbie's father has an Irish background. He met their mother in the Royal Canadian Air Force, and the family lived in various parts of Canada. Gerry, who was born in Saskatchewan, came to Toronto in the 1970s. After some two decades with the CBC, she has now established herself as a successful freelance film make-up artist. Bobbie was born in Winnipeg and came to Toronto in the 1960s. She works on aboriginal social and economic development issues, and has wider interests in new forms of social housing. All told, according to the Canadian federal census, there were approximately forty thousand people of aboriginal descent in the Greater Toronto Area in 1991.

Susanne Milligan, Photographer

Select Bibliography

Allen, Robert Thomas. *When Toronto Was for Kids.* Toronto: McClelland and Stewart, 1961.

Bruce, Jean. *Back the Attack! Canadian Women During the Second World War— At Home and Abroad.* Toronto: Macmillan of Canada, 1985.

Callaghan, Morley. *Strange Fugitive.* Toronto: Macmillan of Canada, 1928, 1973.

Careless, J.M.S. *Toronto to 1918: An Illustrated History.* Toronto: James Lorimer & Company, 1984.

Dickson, Lovat. *Grey Owl: Man of the Wilderness.* Toronto: Macmillan of Canada, 1976.

Glazebrook, G.P. de T. *The Story of Toronto.* Toronto: University of Toronto Press, 1971.

Guillet, Edwin C. *Pioneer Settlements in Upper Canada.* Toronto: University of Toronto Press, 1933, 1969.

Harney, Robert F. (ed.). *Gathering Place: Peoples and Neighbourhoods of Toronto, 1834–1945.* Toronto: Multicultural History Society of Ontario, 1985.

Hill, Lawrence. *Women of Vision: The Story of the Canadian Negro Women's Association.* Toronto: Umbrella Press, 1996.

Innis, Mary Quayle. *Unfold the Years: A History of the Young Women's Christian Association in Canada.* Toronto: McClelland and Stewart, 1949.

_________ (ed.). *Mrs. Simcoe's Diary.* Toronto: Macmillan of Canada, 1965.

Jameson, Anna. *Winter Studies and Summer Rambles in Canada.* Toronto: McClelland and Stewart, 1838, 1966.

Kennedy, Betty. *Hurricane Hazel.* Toronto: Macmillan of Canada, 1979.

Lemon, James. *Toronto Since 1918: An Illustrated History.* Toronto: James Lorimer & Company, 1985.

Ondaatje, Michael. *In the Skin of a Lion.* Toronto: McClelland and Stewart, 1987.

Precourt, Geoffrey and Anne Faircloth. "Best Cities: Where the Living Is Easy." *Fortune.* November 11, 1996.

Robinson, Percy. *Toronto During the French Regime, 1615–1793.* Toronto: University of Toronto Press, 1933, 1965.

Smith, Goldwin. *Canada and the Canadian Question.* Toronto: University of Toronto Press, 1891, 1973.

Sobel, David, and Susan Meurer. *Working at Inglis: The Life and Death of a Canadian Factory.* Toronto: James Lorimer & Company, 1994.

Speisman, Stephen A. *The Jews of Toronto: A History to 1937.* Toronto: McClelland and Stewart, 1979.

Steckley, John. "Toronto: What Does It Mean?" *Arch Notes.* May/June 1992.

White, Randall. *Too Good to Be True: Toronto in the 1920s.* Toronto: Dundurn Press, 1993.

_________ and David Montgomery. *Who Are We? Changing Patterns of Cultural Diversity on the North Shore of Lake Ontario.* Toronto: Waterfront Regeneration Trust, 1994.

Wilson, Barbara M. (ed.), *Ontario and the First World War 1914–1918: A Collection of Documents.* Toronto: University of Toronto Press, 1977.

Women's Press Collective, *Women at Work: Ontario, 1850–1930.* Toronto: Canadian Women's Educational Press, 1974.

Index of Photographs

Agnes Macphail whispers in Mitch Hepburn's ear, June 19, 1941, 82
Alex MacDonald's women's movement, Lynd Avenue, 1991, 128
Alice Dinnick, wife of Augustus George Dinnick, early 1900s, 18
Annemarie Smith on her brother's motorcycle, 1971, 112
Armistice day in Toronto, November 11, 1918, 38
At Queen's Park, September 14, 1945, 89
At the Heliconian Club in Yorkville, 1950s, 97
At Maharani Fashions on Gerrard Street, 1997, 132
At the Women's Press, ca. 1979, 118

Barbara Elizabeth Mercer, as a young woman, late 1950s, 101
Baby Clinic at St. Christopher House, First World War, 37
Betty Kennedy and friend, CFRB, early 1970s, 110
Bill Nix returns from the Great War in Europe, 1919, 39
Blossom Time at the Royal Alex, May 9, 1941, 84
Breaking the glass ceiling at the city of North York, 1980, 119

Cabinet ministers' wives, Ontario Farmer-Labour government, ca. 1920, 44
Canadian Red Cross and Ford Ambulance, ca. 1915, 34
Caribbean Toronto meets Mediterranean Toronto in the 1990s, 127
Chinese celebration, Miss Mary Lee, Toronto, October 18, 1928, 55
Cigarette girls, Royal Regiment dance, October 3, 1941, 79

Departing Toronto soldier with girl's picture in hat, ca. 1916, 33
Domestic science class, old Technical School, ca. 1910, 24
Doreen Messias, Sunnyside Easter parade, early 1950s, 95
Doris Anderson and the staff at *Chatelaine*, 1972, 109

Fashion file at the CNE, mid- to late-1960s, 107
Flower sellers at Italian picnic, August 1, 1932, 62
Flowers in May on the Danforth, ca. 1910, 23
Flowers on the Danforth in the 1990s, 120

Gerry and Bobbie, two sisters in the GTA today, late summer 1997, 141
Grannies' tug of war, Centre Island, ca. 1908, 21
Grecian dancers in conservatory fountain, August 24, 1925, 52

Her Worship Barbara Hall, last mayor of the old city of Toronto, 1996, 135
Hikers, Eglinton Avenue West, near Bathurst Street, 1912, 28
Home-front glamour girl and hoops, Kiwanis Karnival, September 2, 1942, 74

Immigrant woman and child, mid-1900s, 19
I'm not married, August 14, 1945, 88
Isobel Hoffmann: Toronto Woman Entrepreneur of the Year, 1997, 129
Italian banquet hall, 1960s, 102

Jamaican wedding, July 29, 1926, 51
Jeanette Lastowska, Miss Toronto Argonaut 1951, 90
Jewish girls at the Toronto Lakefront, mid- to late-1900s, 22
John Boyd and his fiancée, Marjorie Lang, Sandy Point, 1925, 15
June Callwood and Trent Frayne, May 2, 1944, 86
Junior League Cabaret, March 6, 1937, 67

Kensington Market in the early 1980s, 122
Kensington Market, July 15, 1926, 54
Kew Beach paddlers, 1922, 47

Lady Eaton and two daughters at Hunt Club meet, ca. 1930, 61
Lady Godiva and her horse, Peeping Tom, CNE, September 3, 1935, 66
Last pay, munitions workers, southeast corner of King and Dufferin streets, 1918, 36
Little mothers' class, St. Helen's Separate School, October 31, 1919, 41

Madame Justice Rosalie Abella, December 1989, 125
Mae Genno, Miss By-Line 1951, spring 1951, 94
Mail-order office, Robert Simpson Co., ca. 1909, 25
Marilyn Bell surrounded by gifts, 1954, 99
Marilyn Lastman, first lady of the city of North York, 1980s, 123
Mary Pickford and Douglas Fairbanks on a Toronto visit, March 1924, 48
May "Billie" Hallam, Miss Toronto 1937, July 18, 1937, 70

May Day parade, Riverdale Park, May 1, 1935, 63
Mediterranean Toronto at College and Clinton streets, 1980, 117
Miss Jennie Brown, Runnymede area, July 1923, 45
Miss Italia in the World Canada, 1995, 1996, 1997, 126
Miss Aldeane Eagan, ski club masquerade, April 16, 1926, 53
Mona Parker at lathe, Inglis plant, August 24, 1940, 76
Mother and daughter on the Beaches boardwalk, 1990s, 130
Mount Pleasant beauty, May 22, 1940, 78
Mrs. Ambrose Small, will case, April 28, 1924, 49
Ms. Eileen O'Sullivan at Cherry Beach, 1950s, 98
Ms. Michele Landsberg in the early 1950s, 96

Nan Morris, Miss Toronto 1939, and her mother, July 9, 1939, 71
Nora Vaughan in her sixties, in the 1960s, 108
Nude model at Ontario School of Art, The Grange, ca. 1920, 42

On the waterfront at Fisherman's Island, Toronto, ca. 1907, 16
On the waterfront at Balmy Beach, summer 1997, 136
Ontario Jockey Club, 1913, 27
Opening day at the Club Esquire, Lakeshore Road at Parkside Drive, November 26, 1936, 65
Opening of skating rink, new City Hall, November 29, 1964, 106

Pamela Wallin and her friend, Kitty, late 1990s, 134
Pupils on relief strike, Danforth Park School, East York, November 12, 1935, 64

Racist signs at Fallingbrook Beach, June 27, 1938, 72
Rain storm at the Canadian National Exhibition, just after the First World War, 30
Raynette Coker, Miss Toronto United Appeal 1973, 114
Rear at 18 William Street, August 28, 1914, 32
Rice Bowl festival, July 11, 1941, 83
Roller-skating, Mutual Arena, late 1940s, 93

Sally Lee Orchestra, concert at Christie Street Hospital, January 21, 1938, 58
Saying goodbye to unemployed Toronto men, leaving for the north, October 1, 1931, 60
Somali Shash Sar in North York, summer 1997, 131
Suhana Meharchand and friend, Fairview Mall, 1970, 111
Suki Ulman, giving peace a chance on Indian Road, 1975, 115

The YWCA's "Ontario House," mid- to late-1900s, 20
The Datten family's new bungalow, Silverthorn, 1921, 46
The Braithwaite family on their way home from church, 1963, 103
The new woman in politics, Olivia Chow in the summer of 1987, 124
Three women, taking advantage of the great outdoors, late spring, 1940, 81
Three women, taking advantage of the great outdoors, March 23, 1941, 80
Three French-Canadians in their second home, later 1990s, 133
Toronto Indian Council Club, March 12, 1938, 69
Toronto girls to Cooksville farm, July 13, 1943, 85
Twin sisters, 1976, 116

U of T women's hockey team, Victoria College rink, ca. 1912, 26

VE Day on Bay Street, May 7, 1945, 87

Waiting for Honest Ed, Bloor and Bathurst, 1970s, 104
War widows, ca. 1920, 40
Wartime aviation in Toronto, ca. 1916, 35
Willard Hall, Toronto, Women's Christian Temperance Union, June 17, 1929, 56
Winsome McFarlane and Thor, Rochdale College, 1972, 113
Woman smoking cigar, February 16, 1937, 68
Woman waving nylon stockings, February 19, 1946, 92
Women in the Royal Canadian Air Force, War Loan parade, September 10, 1940, 77
Women eating lollipops, 1911, 29
Women photographers, Toronto Normal School, 1922, 8
Women's fashions at the Don Jail, 1950s, 100
Women's Olympic team leaves Union Station, May 1928, 57
Women's Auxiliary, Old Mount Sinai Hospital, ca. 1939, 73

Young ladies judging domestic science, CNE, September 9, 1925, 50